People and Life 3

People and Life 3

Author Jack McBain
Publisher Chung Kyudo
Editors Kwak Bitna, Cho Sangik
Designers Park Bohee, Lee Seunghyun

First Published January 2018
By Darakwon Inc.
Darakwon Bldg., 211, Munbal-ro, Paju-si, Gyeonggi-do 10881
Republic of Korea

Tel. 82-2-736-2031 (Ext. 550)

ISBN 978-89-277-0935-0 14740
978-89-277-0932-9 14740 (set)

http://www.darakwon.co.kr

Main Book / Free MP3 Available Online
9 8 7 6 5 4 3 24 25 26 27 28

People and Life 3

Introduction

People and Life 3 is the third book in a four-level series for adult and young adult learners of English. This dynamic series contains material appropriate for students ranging from a beginning level to an intermediate level. Each book in the series provides more challenging material in order to meet the linguistic needs of a diverse community of language learners.

People and Life 3 has 12 units, each of which consists of a warm-up, 4 supporting lessons, and a wrap-up, which serves as a review of the unit. The book covers a variety of topics set in a Western sociocultural context. Students will find topics such as stress, dating, and healthy life habits interesting and relevant. Topics that are accessible and relevant to a student's life make learning English easier and more fun.

As a multi-skill course book, *People and Life 3* introduces essential everyday English with speaking, listening, writing, reading, grammar, and vocabulary sections. However, the speaking and listening sections have been emphasized due to the critical importance of these two language skills. *People and Life 3* offers numerous opportunities for students to engage in conversations and participate in activities in English. Through these interactive, confidence-gaining, and interesting activities, students can develop their communication skills and make progress toward greater competence in English.

Author's Acknowledgments

The author would like to express his most sincere gratitude to the editor Bitna Kwak. Without her tireless work and guidance, this project would not have been possible. He would also like to acknowledge the contributions of the Darakwon management and staff. Finally, he would like to extend a heartfelt thanks to his family, who has been incredibly patient during the writing process of this book.

Scope and Sequence

Unit	Learning Outcomes	Speaking
Unit 1 Life and Learning p.11 Orientation Day A Club Meeting Lai plays chess on Saturdays. First Impressions	*Students can . . .* talk about university majors talk about activities they are good at / not good at say when they do certain activities talk about first impressions	Items roommates need for a new place When people do certain activities First impressions Professional goals for the future
Unit 2 Stress p.21 He keeps giving me his work! The baby's crying. You could have done it then. Healthy Life	*Students can . . .* talk about problems at work talk about stressful situations describe people using *so* and *such* talk about busy schedules talk about deadlines talk about how to deal with stress	Annoying office personality types A stressful event Using *so* and *such* Future intentions and deadlines
Unit 3 Entertainment p.31 Can you help me download it? Do you like comedies? A Sports Podcast The New Radio	*Students can . . .* make polite requests talk about movies ask polite questions recommend a movie	Making polite requests Guessing movie titles A movie recommendation
Unit 4 Conflict p.41 I totally disagree! I've got a big problem. It's so annoying! Break Room Memos	*Students can . . .* agree and disagree ask for and give opinions give an opinion about an annoying situation give advice	Agreeing and disagreeing What should I do? Which situation is the most annoying?
Unit 5 Fashion and Personal Style p.51 I want to go to the outlet mall. I need a new look. Can I borrow your red vest? Three Years Ago vs. Now	*Students can . . .* talk about shopping bargain for goods describe their wardrobes and style make fashion suggestions for certain occasions talk about how someone's lifestyle has changed	Buying and selling items My style What should he/she wear? My wardrobe A good bargain
Unit 6 Immigration and Life Abroad p.61 Have you gotten your visa yet? I heard you got your green card.	*Students can . . .* have a conversation with an airport customs official talk about living and working abroad describe other countries describe their jobs	Going through customs Working abroad My job Creating a new country

Grammar	Listening	Vocabulary	Reading / Writing
be + adjective + at adverbials of time	New roommates University clubs A campus festival First impressions	University majors	**Reading** *First Impressions*
so and *such* *by* and *until* *for*, *while*, and *during*	Work problems A stressful weekend A school project which is due soon	Annoying office personality types Words related to stress and stressful situations	**Reading** Why stress is bad for your health
Polite requests and imperatives Embedded questions	An argument at a comedy show A conversation about movies Helping a friend set up an OnTube channel	Movie genres	**Reading** Podcasting **Writing** A favorite form of entertainment
	Speakers agreeing and disagreeing with one another Solving a scheduling conflict Expressing opinions in conversations A recurring problem at work	Annoying habits	**Reading** *Break Room Memos* **Writing** An advice column
	A garage sale A large discount A flea market Three people describing their styles Dressing inappropriately for a date	Shopping expressions Fashion words and expressions	**Reading** Maria's Blog **Writing** How a classmate's lifestyle has changed in the past three years
	Studying abroad Applying for a temporary work visa Three people talking about their jobs	Travel and immigration	**Reading** *Tips for Living Abroad* **Writing** A country you would like to live and work in

Getting Ready

Let's learn some useful classroom expressions.

Your teacher says . . .

Find a partner.
Get into groups of three/four/etc.
Stand up and mingle. Then ask your classmates the questions.
Share your opinions/ideas.
Present your ideas to the group/class.

Students give advice and share opinions . . .

I think . . .
I think you / we should . . .
In my opinion, we should . . .
If I were you, I would . . .
Why don't you / we . . . ?
I totally agree with you.
I strongly disagree.

Unit 1

Life and Learning

Warm-up

Match the pictures to the correct comments.

1. 

2. 

3. 

4. 

5. 

a. "Great party, Andrew! Thank you for inviting us!"

b. "Today, we're going to sing *My Favorite Thing*. Are you ready? Then let's sing... One more time from the top!"

c. "*Bonjour*! I'm so glad to hear that you joined our club. I hope we have some fun while learning French."

d. "Um... it seems that you've had quite a long break. It's been almost a year. Can you tell me what you did during the break?"

e. "Welcome to G&E, Inc. Today, we are holding a brief orientation in order to share some information about our company with you..."

Orientation Day

Conversation

Listen and practice the conversation. 01-01

A Excuse me, but do you know where Winslow Hall is?

B I'm heading there right now. I can take you.

A Thanks.

B I'm Karin, by the way. What's your name?

A I'm Jim. It's nice to meet you.

B It's nice to meet you too, Jim. Are you a freshman?

A Yes, I am. I'm supposed to attend the orientation at 1:00 p.m. But I got lost. The campus is so big!

B I know. I got lost all the time last year. I'm a sophomore now. I'm actually working at the orientation this afternoon. What's your major?

A Engineering.

B Great! I'm supposed to give the engineering students a tour of the campus as part of the orientation. I'll be your group leader.

A I'm so glad I asked you for directions.

Vocabulary

Write the common university majors in the correct places.

biology psychology chemistry accounting
philosophy journalism electronic engineering history

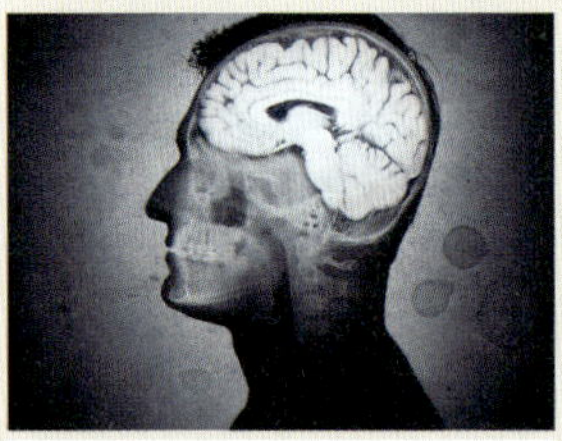

1.

the study of the human mind and the reasons for people's behavior

2.

the study of how to keep track of a company's financial information

3.

the study of reporting the news and writing news articles

4.

the study of life and living organisms

5.

the study of the way that elements react with other substances

6.

the study of electricity, electronics, and electromagnetism

7.

the study of the nature of existence, knowledge, and thought

8.

the study of events that happened in the past

Listening

A Listen to the conversation and answer the questions. 01-02

1. Who are Elena and Kelly?
   a. friends b. colleagues c. roommates
2. What is Kelly's major?
   a. She doesn't have one. b. psychology c. game design
3. What can be inferred from the conversation?
   a. Kelly and Elena haven't met before.
   b. Elena is going to choose the same major as Kelly.
   c. Kelly and Elena are going to be neighbors.
4. What will Kelly and Elena do next?
   a. They will meet other students on the same floor.
   b. They will get something from Kelly's car.
   c. They will buy a television.

B Listen again and choose True or False.

1. Elena does not have a major right now. [True / False]
2. Elena chose a bed before Kelly. [True / False]
3. Kelly brought a printer. [True / False]
4. The women live in an apartment. [True / False]

Pair Work

A Imagine you and your partner are going to share an apartment. You need one of each of the items below for the room. Talk to your partner and decide who will bring which items.

Items	Student A	Student B
Television	17-inch television	32-inch television
Computer	desktop P.C.	none
Microwave	3-month-old microwave	5-year-old microwave
Stereo System	none	stereo system with 2 speakers
Printer	black and white printer	color printer
Video Game Console	2012 video game console	2017 video game console

A Do you have a television?
B Yes, I do. I have a thirty-two-inch television.
A I have a seventeen-inch television. So you should bring yours.
B Okay. Sounds good!

B What other items do you think you need?

A Club Meeting

Conversation

Listen and practice the conversation. 01-03

A Martin, are you interested in joining Speech Masters?
B Speech Masters? What's that?
A It's a speech club.
B I don't know. I'm not very good at public speaking.
A That's the point. The club will help you improve your public speaking skills.
B When does the club meet?
A It meets twice a week on Tuesdays and Thursdays at 5:30 p.m.
B Hmm. I guess I could go to the meeting this Thursday. Maybe I'll like it.
A Great. I'll put your name on the list.
B How many members are there?
A We have nine regular members, but we'd like to have more.

Useful Expressions

A Let's learn some useful expressions.

be + adjectives + at	
I'**m good at** playing the guitar. Yung **is skilled at** fixing cars. Steve and Amy **are talented at** playing soccer.	I'**m not good at** finding locations. Aoki **is bad at** making friends. She's too shy. Pedro and Martin **are poor at** speaking Japanese.

B Write true sentences about yourself by using the keywords in the table.

1. Speaking English *I'm good at speaking English.*
2. Rapping ______
3. Drawing portraits ______
4. Hiding your feelings ______
5. Making people laugh ______
6. Giving presentations ______
7. Taking photographs ______

Listening

A Listen to the conversation and answer the questions. 01-04

1. What clubs was the woman a member of at her university?
   a. tennis and choir b. badminton and guitar c. badminton and choir

2. Who does the woman play badminton with?
   a. her friend b. her husband c. the choir members

3. How many nights a week was the man involved in school clubs?
   a. three nights a week
   b. four nights a week
   c. five nights a week

4. What can be inferred about the woman?
   a. She is going to perform this Sunday morning.
   b. She joined the badminton club because she was talented at it.
   c. She occasionally sings at a community center.

5. What can be inferred about the man?
   a. He enjoys physical activities.
   b. He enjoys intellectual pursuits.
   c. He enjoys debating with the woman.

B Listen again and check the correct days of the week the woman sings with the choir. Then check how often the man uses math at his job.

	Sun	Mon	Tue	Wed	Thu	Fri	Sat
Woman							
Man							

Lai plays chess on Saturdays.

Useful Expressions

A Let's learn about adverbials of time.

Adverbials of Time
on Mondays, Tuesdays, Wednesdays... He cleans his room on Sundays. **every morning / afternoon / evening** Yumi goes jogging every morning. **once / twice / three times... a day / week / month / year** Michaela and I have piano lessons twice a month.

B Let's make sentences using the presented keywords.

Lai | on Saturdays

1.

Paul and Elizabeth | every morning

2.

Simon and Jane | three times a week

3.

the students | on weekdays

4.

Harold | twice a day

5.

Mariel | most evenings

Lai plays chess on Saturdays.

Listening

A Listen to the conversation and answer the questions. 01-05

1. What are the man and woman talking about?
   a. a house party　　b. a school event　　c. a graduation ceremony
2. What kind of food was NOT served at the festival?
   a. popcorn　　b. cotton candy　　c. hot dogs
3. Who opened for G-Luv?
   a. a new male rapper　　b. a new female singer　　c. a new female rapper

B Listen again and choose True or False.

1. The woman organized the festival. [True / False]
2. There were games with prizes at the festival. [True / False]
3. They only served alcoholic drinks at the festival. [True / False]
4. A famous artist opened for Angel Ramirez. [True / False]
5. The man plans to go to the next festival. [True / False]

Pair Work

Who do you think...?

Read about the four people and guess which person does each of the activities in the table the most often. Take turns by asking and answering questions.

cooks at home	orders takeout food	cleans the house
argues with co-workers	goes to the gym	sleeps late on the weekend

I am Hiro. I am kind of a stay-at-home type. I hardly ever eat out. I love to enjoy a meal in a comfortable atmosphere. And the most comfortable place in my opinion is my home!

I am Mina. I can't stand messes or dirt. My friends think I am too obsessive about cleanliness. But I really love to try out new cleaning supplies. I know you think I'm a little weird, but it relaxes me!

I am Patrick. Actually, I am not very satisfied with my work. I've always wanted to work by myself, but at my current job, I have to work with other people quite often. Sometimes I feel like I just want to quit my job and get a new one! On weekends, I am totally exhausted and sleep all day long.

I am Julian. I do my best to live healthfully. I am a freelance reporter, so I have enough time to exercise every day. That's a huge advantage of my job. I also try to eat only organic food. I think health is the most important thing of all!

A Who do you think cooks at home the most often?
B I think Julian cooks at home the most often because he likes healthy food.

First Impressions

Reading

Read the article. 01-06

First Impressions

by Jennifer Hollands

We have all heard the expression "You never get a second chance to make a first impression." But how true is this age-old saying? Jacob Millibrand, a business expert and life coach, says that we should trust our first instinct because it is often the correct one. He believes this skill was developed in humans many thousands of years ago when people were hunter-gatherers. Humans needed to react quickly to dangrous situations like lion or bear attacks. Our ability to judge situations quickly is one of the reasons why humans have been so successful as a species. Millibrand believes we can use this natural skill to find success in the business world and the relationship world. He tells his clients not to ignore their feelings but to use them in a positive way. If you meet someone and you get a bad feeling about that person, ask yourself why. Perhaps there's a perfectly good reason why the person you have just met makes you feel uncomfortable.

On the other hand, Millibrand recomomends that we not put all of our eggs in one basket. If we put too much stock into first impressions, we might make a mistake and miss out on a good business or relationship opportunity. For example, Millibrand says, if you skip breakfast one morning and then attend a meeting where you are introduced to new people, you could mistake your hunger for other people's bad first impressions. Now you have missed out on a good business or relationship opportunity because you were not in touch with your own feelings. Millibrand believes that if we first learn how to get in touch with our own feelings, our ability to judge the first impressions of others becomes much stronger.

*put much stock into = to trust or to give value to

Comprehension Check Answer the questions about the article.

1. What does Jacob Millibrand believe is often true about a first impression?
2. Why does Jacob Millibrand believe humans developed the ability to judge first impressions?
3. What does Jacob Millibrand tell his clients not to do with their feelings?
4. What can happen if a person puts too much stock in a first impression?
5. How can we become better at judging first impressions?

Listening

Listen to the three conversations and say which person you think made the best first impression and which person made the worst first impression. 01-07

Sandy Leah Lima
Accountant

Personal Information
Date of birth: March 1st, 1990
Nationality: the USA

Contact
Phone: +1 645 384 2342
Email: Leahlima@lrepsne.net

Language
English and French

Education
BA in economics from Rudma College

Work Experience
Worked as an accountant at the Nullan Company from 2016 to 2017

Ted Griffin
Salesman

Personal Information
- Date of birth: June 23rd, 1985
- Nationality: Australia

Contact
- Phone: +61 6223 484 214
- Email: Griffin85@asdnin.com

Language
English and German

Education
BA in German literature from Austro University
Master of Business Administration from Stuart University

Work Experience
Padone Manufacturing (2013-2014)
Internship in Sales Department
ABE, Inc. (2014-2016)
Worked as a salesman

Elliot Johnson
Graphic Designer

- **Personal Information**
Date of birth: December 15th, 1981
Nationality: Mexico
- **Contact**
Phone: +52 1 33 23142352
Email: ElliotJohnson@deaplefle.net
- **Language**
English and Spanish
- **Education**
BA in design from Muenong Art College
- **Work Experience**
George Graphic, Inc. (2013-2014)
Worked as an assistant designer
Milkin Game Company (2015-2017)
Worked as a graphic designer
Developed the popular game *Fish Catcher*

Speaking

A Answer the questions by using your own information.

- What is your major?
- Why did you choose your major?
- What do you see yourself doing professionally in five years? How about in ten years?

B Simulate a job interview and introduce yourself to your interviewer.

Hi. My name is Sabrina Johnson. I am a student at Capital University. My major is English literature. I really love reading novels. My favorite writer is Charles Dickens. Five years from now, I see myself working as an editor for a large publishing company. I want to work with talented authors and help them improve their manuscripts. In ten years, I hope to publish my own novel.

Wrap-up

A Read the sentences and write the correct words in the blanks.

accounting	journalism	philosophy	psychology	electronic engineering

1. Esther is reading *Socrates and Plato* in her ______________ class.
2. Joe does all the ______________ in his after school club. He counts the money and balances the budget.
3. Jin's father writes articles for the city's newspaper. He studied ______________ in college.
4. Beth's major is ______________. She hopes to become a family therapist when she finishes school.
5. Amber and Jim both major in ______________. They hope to work for famous tech companies after college.

B Read the sentences and choose the correct words.

1. Alex won a prize at the national basketball competition. He is (bad / skilled) at basketball.
2. Miranda couldn't understand the American customer. She is (not good / good) at speaking English.
3. Junko and Jin are so (not good / talented) at giving speeches that they've been asked to take part in the local speech contest several times.
4. My mom is an art teacher. She is (good / bad) at drawing pictures.
5. He is afraid of water because he is (talented / poor) at swimming.

C Make a group of four students. Then talk to your group members about the pros and cons of your major and what kind of jobs there are related to your major.

D Go online and search for promising jobs and the requirements for those jobs. Then introduce them to your class.

Unit
2 Stress

Warm-up

A Check the pictures that make you feel stressed.

B What are some positive ways people deal with stressful situations? What are some negative ways people deal with stress?

He keeps giving me his work!

Conversation

Listen and practice the conversation. 02-01

A Courtney, can I talk to you for a moment?

B Sure. What's going on?

A I've got a problem with Carl. He keeps giving me his work.

B What do you mean, Matt?

A At the morning meetings, the manager gives each of us our work for the day. Then, five minutes after the meeting, Carl comes to my desk and asks me to do his work as well!

B Have you discussed this with the manager?

A No, not yet. Carl has worked here a lot longer than me. I don't want to get him in trouble.

B If you're doing your work and Carl's work, what is he doing all day?

A He just hangs out in the breakroom or chats with the executive assistants. Last week, he left early every day. I had to stay late last week just to finish all of the work I had. It's not fair.

B I've worked with Carl for several years. Let me talk to him. Maybe I can get to the bottom of this.

*get to the bottom of (something): to discover the truth about something

Group Work

Annoying Office Personality Types

A Make a group of three to five students. Then look at the following examples of annoying coworkers. What should you do with coworkers like these?

a loud talker

a know-it-all

a bully

a gossip

a lunch thief

a cubicle invader

A What should you do if your coworker is a loud talker?

B I think you should politely ask him or her to speak more quietly.

B What other types of annoying personalities have you experienced at school or work? Share your answers with the group.

A Have you ever experienced any annoying personalities at work?

B Yes, I have. My ex-boss loved to drink. Whenever I went out with him, he wanted me to drink a lot with him and wouldn't let me go home!

Listening

A Listen to the three speakers and answer the questions. 02-02

1. What is Juanita's problem?
   a. Her boss yells at her.
   b. Her boss gives her too much work.
   c. Her boss doesn't pay her enough money.

2. Which person can best relate with Juanita?
   a. someone who has had an argument with his or her boss
   b. someone who doesn't love his or her work
   c. someone who works six days a week

3. How does Mitchell feel about his boss?
   a. He doesn't think she's very intelligent.
   b. He thinks she behaves inappropriately.
   c. He thinks she treats the workers in the office poorly.

4. What can be inferred about Dana?
   a. She feels no need to have a boyfriend.
   b. She thinks interoffice dating is unacceptable.
   c. Her success has made dating difficult.

5. What solution do you think seems the most appropriate?
   a. Juanita needs to use her annual leave and get some rest.
   b. Mitchell should find a new job because of his coworkers.
   c. Dana should love her job more.

B Listen again and choose the correct answers.

1. Juanita's wish is someday to sleep late on (Saturday / Sunday).
2. Mitchell was made the (assistant / project) manager for an important client's business.
3. Dana thinks it's (possible / impossible) to separate one's work life and social life.
4. Dana has had a lot of (career / relationship) success in her life.

Speaking

Talk about a stressful event you experienced within the past month.

I had a test for my driver's license last week. It was really stressful. I was shaking the whole time. I think the instructor felt sorry for me. When it was over, I actually passed. But just by one point!

The baby's crying.

Conversation

Listen and practice the conversation. 02-03

A The baby's crying again.
B Huh? What time is it?
A Three thirty.
B It's so late. Can you see what she wants? I'm so tired.
A So am I. I just fed her an hour ago, so it's your turn.
B But I have to get up early. I've got a really important meeting.
A I need to get up early, too.
B Okay, I'll do it. But what if she won't go back to sleep?
A It'll be fine. She probably just needs a clean diaper. She'll fall asleep right after you change it.
B You're such an optimist. I hope you're right.

Grammar

A Let's learn about *so* and *such*.

so + adjective	such + adjective + noun
I'm **so pleased** to meet you. My husband and I were **so happy** to find this apartment in the city. It's big, and it's near the park. It's **so hot** in here. Please open the window. Erin is **so proud** of her son. He won the spelling bee.	Allison is **such a good sleeper**. Nothing can wake her up. My teacher made **such a big mistake** when he lost the students' tests. Dan's friend is **such a good golfer** that once he got a hole-in-one. Ralph is **such a rude person**!

TIPS & TIPS conjunction *so*

So can also be used as a conjunction.
Allison was tired, ***so*** *she went to bed early.*

B Complete the sentences with *so* and *such*.

1. Don't be ______ grumpy in the morning. Drink some coffee or get more sleep.
2. Stephen Curry is ______ an amazing basketball player.
3. Arianna is ______ a good student. She gets straight A's in every subject.
4. It is cold outside today, ______ don't forget to wear your coat, scarf, and hat.
5. Don't be ______ a downer. At least try to have a good time at dinner tonight.

Pair Work

Read the items below and think of someone you know who fits the description. Then share your answers with your partner.

Think of someone who...

- is such a good singer
- is such a good athlete
- eats so quickly
- is such a good driver
- walks so fast
- talks so loudly
- is such a good English student
- is so creative

A Do you know anyone who sings really well?

B My mom is such a good singer.

Listening

A Listen to the conversation and answer the questions. 02-04

1. Where did Eileen go on Friday evening?
   a. She attended a soccer game.
   b. She went to a recital.
   c. She went to a birthday party.

2. What kind of food did Eileen prepare for the picnic?
   a. She made sandwiches.
   b. She baked a cake.
   c. She prepared a salad.

3. About what age are Jim and his wife's children?
   a. They are elementary school students.
   b. They are teenagers.
   c. They are grownups.

4. How do you think the man feels about his children?
   a. He's glad they are always busy.
   b. He would like to spend more time with them.
   c. He is looking forward to when they go to college.

5. Why do you think the woman is talking to the man?
   a. She needs him to help take care of her children on the weekends.
   b. She is seeking advice about parenting from him because he's a father.
   c. She wants someone who understands her situation to listen to her.

B Listen again and complete the woman's weekend schedule.

	Friday	Saturday	Sunday
A.M.	*Work*		
P.M.			*My Husband's Company Picnic*

You could have done it then.

Conversation

Listen and practice the conversation. 02-05

A Honey, can you watch the kids tonight?
B I'm sorry, but I have to finish this presentation by tonight. I'm giving a presentation at tomorrow's meeting.
A How long have you known about this presentation?
B Since Friday.
A Friday? Why didn't you do it on Friday or yesterday?
B I went to a baseball game on Friday.
A I know. And last night you played billiards with your friends.
B That's true.
A So tonight you're going to watch the kids while I see a movie with my sister. I'll be back by 10:00 p.m. You can finish your presentation then.
B But I won't finish until 3:00 or 4:00 a.m.
A And the next time your boss gives you a task, you won't procrastinate.
B You're right. I guess I'm pulling an all-nighter.

*procrastinate: to put off doing something one needs to do until a later time

Grammar

A Let's learn about *by*, *until*, *for*, *while*, and *during*.

by & until
Guests must RSVP to the wedding invitation **by** July 2nd.
Students have **until** next Wednesday to complete the assignment.

*RSVP is a French phrase, *répondez, s'il vous plaît*, which means "please reply."

for, while, & during
Sarah has known her best friend **for** ten years.
I talked to my sister on the phone **while** I was driving to the store.
The Johnsons had a great time **during** their trip.

B Complete the sentences using *by*, *until*, *for*, *while*, or *during*.

1. I fell asleep _______ reading a book.
2. Pamela has to finish the report _______ the end of the workday on Friday.
3. The students in Ms. Jennings' class had _______ Wednesday to complete the project.
4. Construction workers hate working outside _______ the cold winter months.
5. We've lived in this house _______ 25 years.

C Make sentences using the keywords *by*, *until*, *for*, *while*, or *during*.

John | **finish the project** | tomorrow

1.

Suji | **listened to music** | studying yesterday

2.

Paul | **asked his teacher a question** | class this morning

3.

Demian | **has played the guitar** | three years

4.

You | next Friday | **to submit the report**

John has to finish the project by tomorrow.

Listening

A Listen to the conversation and answer the questions. 02-06

1. What is Barbara's problem?
   a. She missed a deadline in her class.
   b. She has an assignment due the next day.
   c. She forgot to meet her interviewee for her project.
2. When was Barbara's project assigned?
   a. two weeks ago
   b. three weeks ago
   c. one month ago
3. What does Barbara have to do?
   a. She has to interview someone and write a report.
   b. She has to write a report about her diet and exercise habits.
   c. She has to give a presentation about someone's diet and exercise routine.
4. How will Carla help Barbara with her report?
   a. She will write the report for Barbara on her computer.
   b. She will let Barbara use her computer to finish the report.
   c. She will let Barbara use her as the subject of her project.
5. What will Carla do next?
   a. She will call one of her friends to ask for help with Barbara's project.
   b. She will prepare herself for an interview.
   c. She will ask Barbara to meet tomorrow morning.

B Listen again and find the incorrect information in the sentences. Then change the sentences to make them correct.

1. Barbara has already started the project.
2. Barbara put off doing the assignment for days.
3. Barbara has to interview a person about his or her habits.
4. Barbara is going to interview Carla's friend.

Reading

Read the book summary. 02-07

www.HealthyLife.com/book_thestresstest_overview

3 Reasons Stress Is Bad for Your Health

HealthyLife.com editor Tamara Stevenson recently purchased a copy of Evan Handley's book *The Stress Test*. In the book, Handley talks about stress in the modern world. Many of us are running around stressed because our schedules are so busy. We are working, taking care of children, studying, running errands, cleaning, etc. With all of these responsibilities, there is no time left to take care of our health. In the book, Handley outlines three ways stress is destroying our health and why we should avoid stress.

1. Stress destroys your immune system.
When we are stressed, the body's ability to stop illness and diseases decreases. When we are stressed, the body produces a hormone called cortisol. Cortisol actually interferes with the body's natural ability to fight infections. If we can reduce the amount of cortisol, then the body has a better chance of fighting infections, and the recovery times from illnesses are shorter.

2. Stress leads to high blood pressure.
Arteries are the tubes that carry the blood throughout the body. Stress can cause the walls of these tubes to become thicker. When the walls become thicker, it becomes more difficult for blood to travel through the tubes. This forces the heart to work harder and actually makes us feel more tired. Eventually, we end up with high blood pressure. Long-term stress can cause permanent damage to the arteries and the heart. This can lead to a heart attack and even death.

3. Stress is bad for your stomach's health.
Inside everyone's stomach, there are bacteria. Bacteria are actually good for your stomach's health. But some bacteria are bad for your stomach and can cause a lot of problems. Stress actually causes bad bacteria to grow and good bacteria to die. When too much bad bacteria live in your stomach, negative health problems occur. So reducing stress can improve the quality of your stomach's health.

Comprehension Check Answer the questions about the book summary.

1. What kind of article is this?
2. Who wrote the book *The Stress Test*?
3. Why does stress destroy your immune system?
4. Why does stress lead to high blood pressure?
5. Why is stress bad for your stomach?

Survey

A Raise your hand if you feel stressed by the item the teacher reads out loud.

- Giving a speech to a roomful of people
- Taking an exam
- Driving a car
- Talking to a stranger
- Flying on an airplane
- Asking a person out on a date
- Interviewing for a job
- Starting a new job / class
- Meeting your boyfriend's or girlfriend's parents
- Speaking English to a native speaker
- Performing in front of a group of people (acting, singing, etc.)

B Which item resulted in the most students raising their hands?

Wrap-up

A Write the correct office personality in the blanks.

bully	loud talker	gossip	know-it-all	cubicle invader	lunch thief

1. Jane can't keep a secret! She is such a ______________.
2. I can't concentrate on my work because Bob is such a ______________.
3. My boss is a ______________. He intimidates his employees and treats them disrespectfully.
4. Erica is a ______________. She just takes anyone's food from the refrigerator. It's so annoying!
5. John thinks he's an expert about everything. He's a ______________.
6. Youngjin is a ______________. She comes into my workspace far too often.

B Look at the pictures and make sentences using *so* and *such*.

1.

hot / over 40 degrees

2.

dancers / won a dance contest

3.

good at surfing / every summer

4.

workaholic / works over 80 hours a week

C Read the sentences and choose the correct answers.

1. My boss wants the report finished (for / by) 2:00 p.m. on Thursday.
2. The teacher gave her students (while / until) the following week to finish the project.
3. Jacob and his wife used their smartphones (for / during) the trip.

D Read about the stressful situations below and check the ones you have experienced. Then talk to your partner in detail about one of them.

1.	I spilled coffee on my white shirt on my way to work in the morning.	
2.	While flying on an airplane, a baby next to me kept crying.	
3.	I have until tomorrow morning to finish the huge project, and there isn't enough time.	
4.	My coworker talks too much during work, so I can't concentrate.	
5.	I can't sleep on Sunday mornings because of the noisy construction in my neighborhood.	

E Do you have any advice on how to deal with stress? If you do, please share your advice with the class.

Unit 3 Entertainment

Warm-up

A Do you enjoy entertainment by yourself or with other people?

B Rank your top three kinds of entertainment. Then tell your partner why you chose them as your top three.

Can you help me download it?

Conversation

Listen and practice the conversation. 03-01

A Have you listened to the new U2 album yet?
B Not yet. How is it?
A It's amazing. You have to download it.
B How much is the album?
A You can get it at the online music store for $9.99.
B That's not bad. But I don't know how to use the online music store. Can you help me download it?
A Sure. Get your credit card, and I'll help you download it.
B Thanks. Here's my card.

Grammar

A Let's learn about making polite requests from imperatives.

Can / Could + you + verb (infintive) ~?
Can you help me?
Could you please **not call** here after nine o'clock?
Could you please **turn** the music down?
Can you give Andrew my phone number?
Could you tell Yumiko to meet us at the bus stop?
Can you please **stop** teasing your younger sister?

TIPS & TIPS Imperatives

The imperative mood uses the infinitive form of the verb without *to*.

B Look at the pictures. Then decide whether the imperative or the polite request is the most appropriate for each situation.

1.

a. Give me your phone number.
b. Could I have your phone number?

2.

a. Could you please turn off your cell phone?
b. Turn off your cell phone!

3.

a. Can I have a cup of coffee?
b. Give me a cup of coffee.

4.

a. Can I borrow some money?
b. Give me some money.

Pair Work

A Make a list of four imperatives. Then change them into polite requests.

	Imperatives	Polite Requests
	Lend me your phone.	*Could you lend me your phone?*
1.		
2.		
3.		
4.		

B Role-play the polite requests with a partner. Have your partner respond to your polite requests.

A Could you lend me your phone?

B Sure. Here you are.

Listening

A Listen to the conversation and answer the questions. 03-02

1. Where is the couple?
   a. at a movie theater
   b. at a concert
   c. at a comedy show
2. What does the man want to do?
   a. record a performer
   b. copy a movie
   c. take a picture
3. How does the woman feel?
   a. tired b. annoyed c. jealous
4. Where does the woman want to go?
   a. to her house b. to a hotel c. to the car
5. What can be inferred from the conversation?
   a. The man has his own UTube channel.
   b. The woman has recorded a show before.
   c. Both of them are upset.

B Listen again and answer True or False.

1. The man wants to do something illegal. [True / False]
2. The man's phone isn't working. [True / False]
3. People need permission to record a performance and to post it online. [True / False]
4. The performer said the man could record the performance. [True / False]

Do you like comedies?

Conversation

Listen and practice the conversation. 03-03

A What should we see?
B I don't know. Do you like horror movies?
A No, I hate them. They're so silly. They're not even scary.
B Okay, I see. How do you feel about science fiction?
A I'm not really into sci-fi either. What about a romance movie?
B Romance? Yuck!
A Well, what genre do you like?
B I like comedies.
A But I like romance. How about a romantic comedy?
B Hmm. Let's see. There's a romantic comedy starring Adam Sandler starting in 10 minutes.
A Great. Let's buy the tickets and some popcorn.
B Okay!

Vocabulary

Write the movie genres in the correct places.

action	comedy	historical drama	crime drama
horror	romance	science fiction	Western

1.

2.

3.

4.

5.

6.

7.

8.

Listening

Listen to the conversations and answer the questions. 03-04

1-2

1. Why didn't the woman like the ending?
   a. She wanted the superhero to win.
   b. She would have liked the superhero to lose.
   c. She thought the ending was too sad.
2. The woman wants to see a superhero movie where the hero loses. [True / False]

3-5

3. What kind of Woody Allen movies does the woman like?
   a. She likes his newer films.
   b. She likes his older films.
   c. She does not like Woody Allen films.
4. The woman's favorite Woody Allen film is *Annie Hall*. [True / False]
5. The man's favorite Woody Allen film is *Crimes and Misdemeanors*. [True / False]

6-7

6. What is the woman going to do when a scary part comes up?
   a. She's going to leave the theater.
   b. She's going to hold her boyfriend's hand.
   c. She's going to close her eyes.
7. The man has not seen the movie yet. [True / False]

Group Work

What's the Movie?

A Answer the questions about a movie you have seen.

Keep this a secret!

Movie Name: ______________________

1. What genre is the movie?
2. Where is the movie set?
3. Who is in the movie?
4. What is the movie about?
5. What happens at the end?

B Read the clues in the table starting with number 1. Then let your group members guess the name of your movie.

A It's a comedy. It takes place in New York City. Bill Murray is in it. It's about a team of ghost hunters. In the end, they kill a giant marshmallow man.
B Is the movie *Ghostsbusters*?
A Yes, it is.

A Sports Podcast

Conversation

Listen and practice the conversation. 03-05

A What are you doing?
B I'm setting up some microphones.
A What are the microphones for?
B I'm doing a weekly podcast. I post the files on the school's website. Then, students can download the files and listen to the podcasts.
A What kind of podcast is it?
B It's a sports podcast. I discuss our school's sports teams for an hour once a week.
A Who do you discuss it with?
B I ask a different athlete to join me each week. This week, I'm talking to Antoine Jackson. He's the running back on our football team. He's an all-American athlete. Could you tell me what time it is?
A It's 10:30. When is he coming?
B He's going to be here at 11:00.

Grammar

A Let's learn about embedded questions.

Interrogative when / where / what / why / how + subject + verb	Declarative if / whether / whether or not + subject + verb
She didn't know **when the class starts**. Could you tell me **where the police station is**? Do you know **what the name of the movie is**? Ms. Anderson asked me **why I was absent yesterday**. We have no idea **how we can get there**.	Do you know **if it's going to snow this afternoon**? Can you tell **whether or not Jane is coming to the movie**? Paulo doesn't know **whether the class starts at 7:00 or 7:30**. We have no idea **if Susan and Brian broke up yesterday**. Sam asked me **whether or not I had a pencil he could borrow**.

B Fill in the blanks by using the words presented.

1. "Can you tell me ______________________ (time, the movie, what, starts)?" "It begins in ten minutes."
2. Jake asked me whether or not ______________________ (is coming, Maria, to the party).
3. "Do you know ______________________ (summer vacation, when, begins)?"
   "I'm not sure about that."
4. In math class, I encountered a difficult question. I had no idea ______________________ (how, should, solve, I, it).
5. Our teacher asked us if ______________________ (an extra day, we, needed) to prepare for the test.

Listening

A Listen to the conversation and answer the questions. 03-06

1. What does the man want to do?
   a. He wants to help the woman design her OnTube channel.
   b. He wants to learn how to edit videos.
   c. He wants to create an OnTube channel about video games.

2. What does the man think about the woman's OnTube channel?
   a. He is impressed by the design of the channel.
   b. He thinks it could have been designed better.
   c. He wants to create a nutrition channel just like it.

3. How does the woman edit her videos?
   a. She uses software she borrowed from a friend.
   b. She uses an application that she created.
   c. She edits videos using a video editor app she downloaded.

4. What do you think happened after the talk?
   a. The man created a fitness and nutrition website.
   b. The woman viewed the man's OnTube channel.
   c. They created an OnTube channel together.

B Listen again and choose the correct answers.

1. The woman has a (nutrition and dieting / fitness) OnTube channel.
2. The man is going to review (old / new) video games on his OnTube channel.
3. The woman uses (an analog camera / a phone camera) to make her videos.
4. The woman uses a special (tool / skill), so her phone won't move too much.

Group Work

Write four interesting *wh*-questions in the first column. Then change the direct questions into embedded questions and write them in the second column. Finally, make a group of five students and ask them the embedded questions. Write their answers in the third column.

	Direct Questions	Embedded Questions	Answers
	How much sleep do you get?	*Could you tell me how much sleep you get?*	*I get 7 to 8 hours of sleep per night.*
1.			
2.			
3.			
4.			

The New Radio

Reading

Read the article about podcasting. 03-07

Media Magazine

“Podcasting: The New Radio”

By Khan Sindh

Ten years ago, as terrestrial radio was on the decline, a new medium was emerging: podcasting. Podcasting is a digital medium where a person can record a radio program and then upload the file to the Internet. Unlike radio, where the listener must tune in at a specific time in order to listen to the radio program, a podcast can be downloaded and listened to anytime. The listener only needs an Internet connection and a media device capable of playing MP3 files.

Podcasts exist for just about any topic one can think of. For example, if you are interested in true crime, there are a number of true crime podcasts where the hosts interview crime experts about real criminal cases. The podcast might be a series of shows discussing only one event, or there could be a new topic for each show. Podcasts can be broadcast weekly, biweekly, or even daily. Within the new medium of podcasting, there are very few rules. This newfound freedom, unlike in terrestrial radio, allows broadcasters to find their niche audience. Once a podcaster has found an audience, listenership tends to grow through word of mouth.

Podcasting was thought to be a fad by traditional radio broadcasters. But now even traditional broadcasters understand the power and popularity of podcasting. Some terrestrial radio broadcasters such as comedian Thomas Levinson have moved from radio to podcasting and found great success. Thomas Levinson's WPY podcast is one of the most downloaded podcasts in the United States and continues to grow in listenership. In 2016, Thomas Levinson interviewed the former president in his garage. Levinson transformed his garage into a small podcasting studio when he started his podcast several years ago.

Comprehension Check Answer the questions about the article.

1. What has happened to terrestrial radio over the past ten years?
2. What does a person need to listen to a podcast?
3. What kinds of podcasts are there?
4. Why is it easier for podcasters to find their niche audience than radio broadcasters?
5. Where did Thomas Levinson record his interview with the former U.S. president?

Writing

What is your favorite kind of entertainment? How do you spend your free time entertaining yourself?

Speaking

Imagine you and your friend are going to watch a film together. Choose a movie that you think your friend would enjoy. Complete the information in the table to help you summarize it.

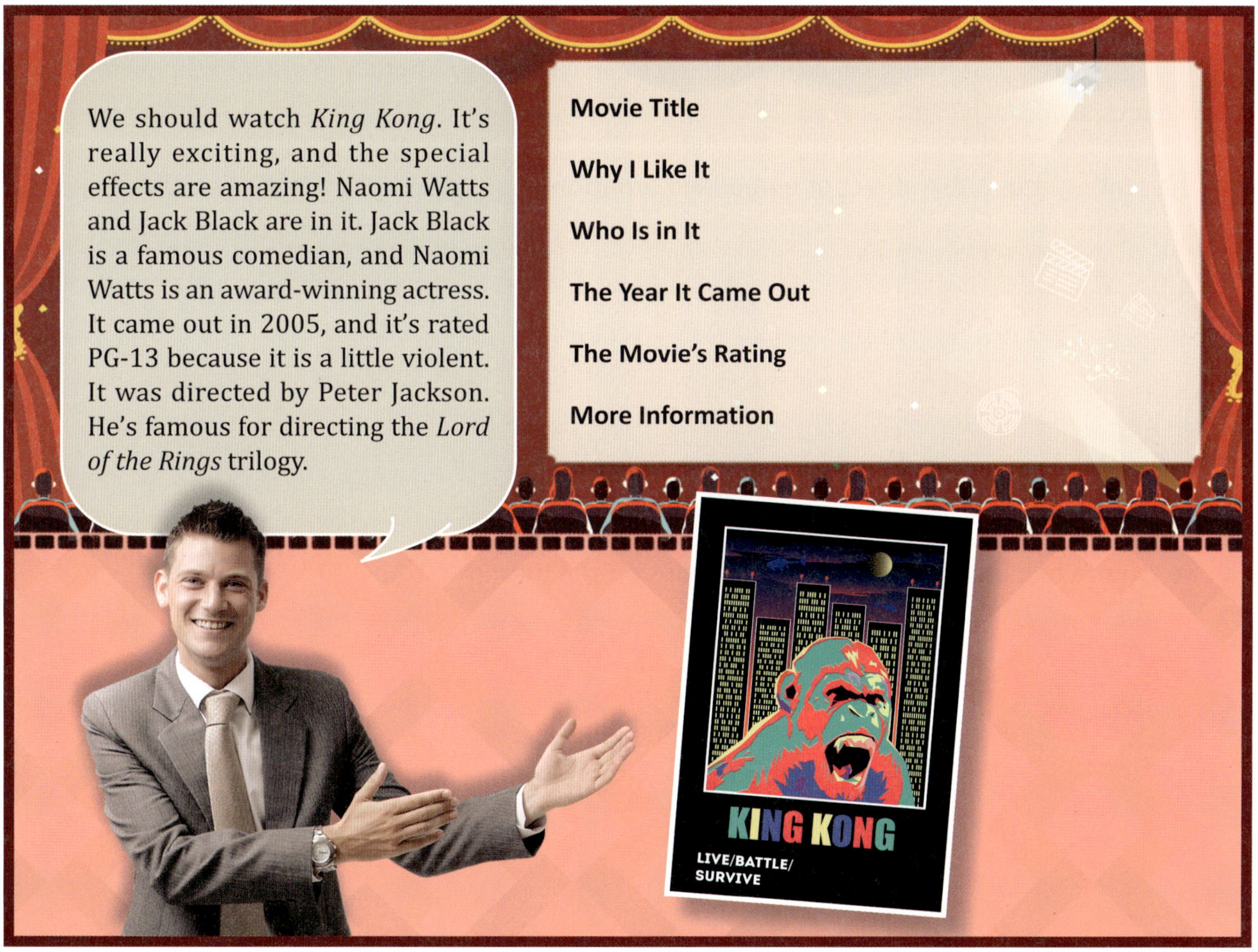

Wrap-up

A Look at the movie scenes and write the appropriate movie genres.

1.

2.

3.

4.

B Fill in the blanks by using the movie genres in A.

1. I am easily frightened, so I don't like watching ______________ movies.
2. April enjoys watching ______________ movies when she is depressed.
3. She occasionally falls in love with an actor in ______________ movies.
4. ______________ scenario writers should study science and technology carefully in order to complete creative but trustworthy movies.

C Rewrite the sentences as either direct or embedded questions.

	Direct Questions	Embedded Questions
1.	*How much water do you drink a day?*	
2.		*Do you know if Bill is coming to the party?*
3.	*Does Alan go to the bank on Tuesdays?*	
4.		*Could you tell me what time it is?*

D Give a one-minute talk using the topic and questions on the prompt card.

Music / Podcasts

- What kind of music / podcasts do you like?
- Why do you like it / them?
- Who is your favorite musician / podcaster?
- When do you listen to it?

E What is your favorite movie genre? And what movie genre is your least favorite? Think about your answers to the two questions and discuss the movie genres you like and dislike.

Unit
4 Conflict

Warm-up

Read the questions and look at the pictures. Then choose the option that you want and make suggestions.

How do you prefer to have your dinner?

In my opinion, we should eat out at a nice restaurant. I feel like some steak.

What would you like to drink with your friends?

Where would you want to go on vacation?

How do you like to watch a movie?

I totally disagree!

Conversation

Listen and practice the conversation. 04-01

A The professor asked us to create a video or to make a presentation. I think we should make a video.

B I'm not so sure about that. I don't know anything about video production.

A I know a lot about making videos. I just finished a video for my English class. The professor loved it.

B But this is a biology class. I think a presentation would be better.

A I'm afraid I disagree. We can be more creative by making a video.

B That's not necessarily true. I've seen some very interesting presentations.

A That's true. But in this case, I really think we should make a video.

B Well, I totally disagree. So what are we going to do?

Useful Expressions

A Let's learn some useful expressions about agreeing and disagreeing.

Agreeing with Someone	Disagreeing with Someone
I totally agree.	I totally disagree.
I couldn't agree more.	I don't think so.
That's so true!	I'm afraid I disagree.
That's for sure!	I beg to differ.
You're absolutely right.	Not necessarily.
Absolutely!	That's not necessarily true.
I feel the same.	That's not necessarily the case.
Exactly!	I'm not so sure about that.

B Read the sentences and fill in the blanks with the letters of the correct responses.

a. That's not necessarily true. b. I'm not so sure about that. c. That's so true.

1. A We should go to the waterpark this weekend.
   B ( ). It's supposed to rain on Saturday.
2. A Running is better exercise than walking.
   B ( ). Walking is better for your joints and muscles.
3. A Children learn languages faster than adults.
   B ( ). My daughter speaks Chinese and English really well.

C Write down your own responses by using the expressions for agreement and disagreement.

A People shouldn't pay money to watch scary horror movies.

B ______________________________

Listening

Listen to the conversations and answer the questions. 04-02

1-2

1. What are the man and the woman going to do on Friday evening?
   a. They are going to have a barbecue.
   b. They are going to go shopping.
   c. They are going to have a dinner party.

2. The man thinks it's too cold for a barbecue. [True / False]

3-5

3. What is the purpose of the conversation?
   a. To make an appointment for an upcoming meeting
   b. To meet clients together
   c. To postpone a meeting until another day

4. The man and woman are going to meet in the afternoon. [True / False]

5. The man is busy on Tuesday morning. [True / False]

6-7

6. What book is the man going to read?
   a. *Firestorm*
   b. *Katherine McKinny*
   c. *Stand Alone*

7. The man and woman disagree about the author. [True / False]

Pair Work

Complete the statements below. Then share your statements with a partner. See if your partner agrees or disagrees with your statements.

The best...
movie genre is _______________.
kind of music is _______________.
ethnic food is _______________.
sport is _______________.
day of the week is _______________.
season is _______________.
time of day is _______________.

A The best movie genre is comedy.
B I totally disagree. The best movie genre is action.

I've got a big problem.

Conversation

Listen and practice the conversation. 04-03

A Hey, Samantha. You look down. What's wrong?
B I've got a big problem.
A What's the problem?
B I saw my roommate's boyfriend having dinner with his ex-girlfriend at a restaurant downtown.
A It's not necessarily as bad as it looks. Maybe they were just talking.
B You're such a typical man. They were holding hands and laughing. It definitely wasn't innocent.
A Hmm. That does sound bad. What are you going to do?
B I don't know. What do you think I should do? Should I tell her, should I talk to him, or should I just stay out of it?
A Honestly, I think she has a right to know. You have to tell her.
B I feel the same way.

Useful Expressions

A Let's learn some useful expressions about asking for and giving opinions.

Asking for an Opinion	Giving an Opinion
What do you think?	In my opinion...
What's your idea?	I think...
What are your thoughts?	If I were you, I would...
How do you feel about that?	If you ask me...
Do you have anything to add?	The way I see it...
Do you agree?	Honestly, I think...
Is there anything else?	As far as I'm concerned...

B Underline the expressions about asking for an opinion and circle the expressions about giving an opinion.

1. A I am going to meet Angela for some pizza and beer. Do you want to join us?
   B Absolutely. How do you feel about going to Queen's Pizza? It just opened last week. I heard from my co-worker that the pizza there tastes great.
   A I know that place. It looks a little expensive though. You told me that you're going to cut back on spending. Honestly, I think we should choose Kim's Pizza Factory.

2. A What do you think about my dress?
   B You look amazing. Where are you going in that fancy dress?
   A I'm not going anywhere. My boyfriend is going to make a video call to me soon.
   B In that case, I think a dress is too much then.

3. A Minji just called me and asked me to go out tonight.
B That sounds great.
A But I have an English test tomorrow...
B If I were you, I would stay home and prepare for the test.

Listening

A Listen to the conversation and complete the information in the wedding invitation. 04-04

Wedding Invitation
Anna Dempsey & Eric Johnson

Date ______________________
Time ______________________
Place ______________________
Guest yes ☐ no ☐
Meal Tomato Pasta ☐ Cream Pasta ☐

B Listen again and choose True or False.

1. Eric Johnson is the man's closest friend. [True / False]
2. The woman's mother's birthday is in June. [True / False]
3. The woman isn't going to the wedding. [True / False]
4. The church is located fifty minutes from where her mother lives. [True / False]

Discussion

Read about the three situations and discuss them with your group. Say whether you agree or disagree with the other group members' opinions.

You and your significant other are at a movie theater. You want to see an action movie, and your significant other wants to see a romantic film. What should you do?

Your best friend borrows your car, but when he / she returns it, there's a scratch on the door. What should you do?

Your professor assigns a group presentation, but one person in the group refuses to do any work. What should your group members do?

A In my opinion, a good boyfriend would let his girlfriend choose the movie. It's the right thing to do.
B I couldn't agree more. A gentleman lets his girlfriend choose the movie. What do you think?
C If you ask me, I think he also has a right to choose the movie he wants to watch.

It's so annoying!

Conversation

Listen and practice the conversation. 04-05

A What's wrong, Min?
B I can't find my stapler.
A Where do you usually keep it?
B On my desk. I keep it next to my computer. I think Janine took it again.
A Let's look on her desk. Oh, here it is.
B It's so annoying! I wish she wouldn't take my stuff without asking.
A I know. She took some files off of my desk the other day and didn't put them back. I looked for them for like half an hour.
B I'm sick of it!
A Me, too. What should we do?
B Let's talk to her when she gets back from lunch.
A Good idea.

Speaking

Look at the pictures. Choose the most annoying situation and say what you think the person should do in the situation.

1.

2.

3.

4.

5.

6.

A The woman's coworkers are too noisy.
B The woman should ask them to speak quietly.

Listening

A Listen to the conversation and answer the questions. 04-06

1. Why was the man late for work?
   a. Traffic was bad.
   b. He overslept.
   c. He left his house too late.

2. When is the man's annual performance review?
   a. It's in a few days.
   b. It's in a few weeks.
   c. It's in a few months.

3. How do you think the man feels?
   a. He is angry with his boss.
   b. He is worried about his job.
   c. He is tired from driving.

4. What do you think Ms. Graves will do if the man is late again?
   a. She will cancel his performance review.
   b. She will send him home.
   c. She will scold him again.

B Listen to the conversation that takes place the next day. Then choose True or False.

1. Philip will start work half an hour earlier. [True / False]
2. Philip lives 60 kilometers from the office. [True / False]
3. Philip's performance review is on the 22nd. [True / False]

Class Activity | Survey about Annoying Habits

A Read the items and check them if they annoy you.

1. Making sounds when having meals ☐
2. Sneezing loudly ☐
3. Nervously tapping one's feet ☐
4. Biting one's nails ☐
5. Going into a room without knocking ☐
6. Wetting one's index finger when turning pages ☐
7. Picking one's nose in public ☐

B Let's see which item is considered the most annoying and which item is the least annoying. When the teacher reads an item you have checked out loud, raise your hand.

Break Room Memos

Reading

Read the three memos. 04-07

Hey, Everyone,

For the second time this week, someone took my sandwich from the refrigerator. I even put my name on the brown paper bag the sandwich was in! This is really annoying because I've had to go out of the office twice this week to buy lunch. I brought sandwiches to work so I wouldn't have to go out. Please be respectful and keep your hands off other people's food. We all have to work together here, so it would be nice if we didn't have to worry about people stealing one another's stuff. Thanks!

Andrea

Dear Employees,

It has come to my attention that some of you have not been cleaning up after yourselves in the breakroom. Several times this week, wrappers, cans, and bottles were left on the tables in the breakroom. I kindly request that you recycle the bottles and cans and throw the wrappers and other trash in the trash can in the breakroom. Let's all pitch in a little bit by throwing away our trash. The evening cleaning crew will really appreciate it. And I would also appreciate it. Thanks!

Dale Robinson
Manager

Attention!

If you use the copy machine and there's a paper jam, don't just go to another machine. Fix the paper jam. If you can't fix the paper jam, call Michael at ext. 1124, and he will help you. If you walk away from the problem and don't tell anyone, the next person to use the machine will have a problem. Please show some good office etiquette. Thank you for your attention!

Randy

Comprehension Check Answer the questions about the memos.

1. What did Andrea do to try to prevent her sandwiches from getting stolen?
2. What did Andrea do when she realized someone had eaten her sandwiches?
3. What should employees do with bottles and cans in the breakroom?
4. When does the cleaning crew clean the office?
5. Who should employees call if there's a problem with the copy machine? What number should they call?

Writing | Dear Amy

Imagine you write an advice column for a newspaper called "Dear Amy." Choose two people to give advice to and write your advice in the spaces at the bottom of the page.

1 Dear Amy,

My boyfriend always looks at other girls while we're out. Can't he see that it hurts my feelings when he does this? What should I do?

Candy

2 Dear Amy,

My brother called me and asked me for some money to pay for damage to his car. He asked me because he didn't want our parents to find out about the accident. What should I do?

Matt

3 Dear Amy,

My friend always wants to go to the bar on the weekend, but whenever I go out with her, she makes me pay for her drinks. She's not my girlfriend, but I still pay for her. I wish she would pay sometimes. What should I do?

Hiroshi

4 Dear Amy,

My boss seems to have a problem with women. At meetings, he only asks the men for their opinions and ideas. He never asks the women even though we have the same positions as the men. What should we do?

Kelly

Dear ____________________,

Sincerely
Amy

Dear ____________________,

Sincerely
Amy

Wrap-up

A Agree or disagree with the following statements.

1. Drinking alcohol is better than drinking coffee when you want to get to know someone.
   I totally disagree. I became close to my best friend without drinking alcohol.
2. Traveling abroad is better than traveling domestically.
3. Taking the subway is more convenient than taking the bus.
4. Working outside is more interesting than working inside.
5. Swimming is healthier than running.

B Give your opinions about the following situations.

1. I'm too tired. What should I do?
   In my opinion, you should go to sleep earlier. Then, you won't be so tired.
2. I think learning English is too difficult. What are your thoughts?
3. I forgot my mother's birthday. What should I do?
4. I don't like summer. It's too hot. How do you feel about summer?
5. My neighbors are too noisy. What should I do?

C Is there any conflict you're having these day? If there is, share it with a partner and ask for advice.

D Search the Internet for articles to find out what kinds of conflicts people generally experience at work or school. Then share them with the class.

Unit 5

Fashion and Personal Style

Warm-up

A What are the people wearing? What activities might they be planning to do in these clothes?

B Describe what you are wearing right now to a classmate.

I want to go to the outlet mall.

Conversation

Listen and practice the conversation. 05-01

A What are you doing this weekend, Stephanie?
B I want to go to the outlet mall in Northridge.
A Northridge is a little far, isn't it?
B It is, but I heard there are some incredible bargains there.
A What kinds of bargains?
B Fall coats were 50% to 70% off last weekend.
A Wow! That's a steal.
B I know. Would you like to go with me this weekend?
A Yes, I would. I need a few new sweaters and maybe a pair of jeans.
B They've got everything. It's all quite cheap because they're last season's designs.
A That's okay. As long as it looks good, I'll buy it.

Vocabulary | Shopping Expressions

Write the words or phrases in the correct places.

an outlet mall	a yard sale	a fitting room	brand name	
a steal	off-brand	e-commerce	a rip-off	a flea market

1.

____

2.

____

3.

____

4.

____

5.

____

6.

____

7.

____

8.

____

9.

____

Listening

A Listen to the conversations and answer the questions. 05-02

1. Where is Clair going to sell the items?
   a. at a yard sale
   b. at a flea market
   c. at an outlet mall

2. Why is the Luis Belvoir handbag 70% off?
   a. It's a generic handbag.
   b. It's last year's design.
   c. It's damaged.

3. How many times has the man been to the Centerville Flea Market?
   a. once
   b. twice
   c. three times

B Write the correct numbers in the blanks.

1.	2.	3.	4.

Matt's age: ________	70% discount price: $ ________	Price: $ ________	Agreed-upon price: $ ________

Pair Work

The Flea Market

Imagine you are at a flea market. Choose two items you want to sell and set your own prices for them. Then try to bargain with your partner by using the information about each item.

 $ ________	• bought in a flea market • unique design • one bead missing • partially rusty	 $ ________	• bought a few months ago • brand-new product • good sound quality • adjustable length cord • small scratches
 $ ________	• bought in 1995 • worn out • one string missing • autographed by Paul McCartney • needs to be tuned	 $ ________	• 100% cashmere • made by a luxury brand • well-preserved • coffee stains on the right sleeve • only dry cleaning

A How much are these earrings?
B They're $2.50.
A How about $2.00? Some of the metal parts are rusty, and one bead is missing.

I need a new look.

Conversation

Listen and practice the conversation. 05-03

A Kenny, do you like these pants?
B Yes, I do. They look great!
A Ugh, I'm not so sure. I'm so tired of my wardrobe.
B Why don't you go shopping and get some new clothes?
A It's not just my clothes. I need a new look. I want to change my style.
B You could get a makeover, too. There's a new hair salon in the strip mall on 4th Avenue.

A You're right. A makeover and a new wardrobe might get me out of this rut.
B Do you want me to give you a ride there?
A Sure. But shouldn't I make an appointment first?
B I don't think they'll be too busy on a Tuesday afternoon.

*get out of a rut: to refresh oneself

Vocabulary | Fashion

A Match the fashion words and expressions with the correct descriptions.

casual / dressed down	vintage	dress for the occasion
~~classic / timeless~~	dressed up	the latest trend
off-the-peg / off-the-rack	thrift store	chic

ex. *classic / timeless* : clothing that never goes out of style

1. ______________ : elegant or very fashionable
2. ______________ : clothing from another time period; out-of-date clothing
3. ______________ : a store that sells used clothing and accessories
4. ______________ : informal clothing; not dressed up
5. ______________ : formal clothing; more than casual dress
6. ______________ : to wear the appropriate clothing for a certain event
7. ______________ : clothing bought from a clothing store that offers the same design in a number of sizes; not a unique design
8. ______________ : the most recent clothing designs

B Use the words or expressions to describe your wardrobe.

I think I have many vintage items. They are cheap and unique, so I can be fashionable by spending less money.

Listening

Listen to the conversations and answer the questions. 05-04

1-2

1. How does Britney describe her style?
   a. casual
   b. thrifty
   c. beautiful

2. Why does Britney wear sleeveless shirts?
   a. It's too hot in her city.
   b. She's conservative.
   c. She likes her arms to be tan.

3-4

3. How many T-shirts does Kyle own?
   a. more than 30
   b. more than 40
   c. more than 50

4. Where did Kyle get his favorite T-shirt?
   a. at an outlet mall
   b. at a thrift store
   c. at a concert

5-6

5. How does Francine feel about wearing glasses?
   a. She hates wearing glasses.
   b. She thinks they look fashionable.
   c. She feels embarrassed.

6. What can be inferred about Francine?
   a. She visits high-end stores very often.
   b. She will not wear her favorite T-shirt until next month.
   c. She often goes to the hair salon to have her hair cut.

Group Work

What's your style?

Look for a picture on your smartphone that best represents your personal style and present your personal style to your group.

Can I borrow your red vest?

Conversation

Listen and practice the conversation. 05-05

A Did you borrow my dark blue skinny jeans?
B Yes, I did. I'm sorry I forgot to tell you.
A I was going to wear them on my date with Todd tonight. But now they're dirty.
B I'm really sorry. Do you want to borrow my black skirt?
A We're just going to a movie, so I don't want to dress up that much. I guess I can wear my black jeans. Can I borrow your red vest?
B Sure. I just picked it up from the dry cleaner.
A Great. I think I'll wear my black boots, too. What do you think?
B Absolutely. The black boots will look great with your black jeans and my red vest.

Speaking | Dressing for the Occasion

Here are Alex and Amanda. Look at the items they have and say how they should dress for each of the occasions below.

1. Amanda has a job interview on Monday morning.
   Amanda should dress up for her interview. She should wear a suit, dress shoes, and a watch.
2. Alex is helping his brother move to a new apartment on Tuesday.
3. Amanda is going to the beach next weekend.
4. Alex is going to meet his client on Thursday morning.
5. Alex and Amanda are going to Amanda's sister's wedding on Saturday.

Listening

A Listen to the conversation and answer the questions. 05-06

1. Why is Mindy upset with her boyfriend Pablo?
   a. He dressed up too much for dinner last night.
   b. He didn't dress up enough for dinner last night.
   c. He wore jeans to dinner last night.

2. How did Mindy dress for her date?
   a. She dressed casually.
   b. She dressed formally.
   c. She wore business casual attire.

3. What most appropriately describes the shift in Mindy's mood last night?
   a. surprised – pleased b. frustrated – furious c. enthusiastic – hurt

4. What can be inferred about Pablo?
   a. He may not want to be controlled by Mindy.
   b. He goes jogging every day.
   c. He doesn't like to wear formal clothes.

B Listen again and change the wrong sentences to make them true.

1. Mindy and Pablo went to dinner on St. Patrick's Day.
2. Mindy and Pablo met at La Grande, the new Italian restaurant.
3. Mindy was very proud of the way Pablo looked at dinner.
4. Mindy thinks Pablo looks handsome in his blue suit.
5. Pablo might think Mindy treats him like an adult.

C What would you do if your partner refused to dress up for a night out in a nice restaurant?

Group Work

A Complete the table with information about your wardrobe.

What is in your wardrobe that you...	
can't live without?	
like a lot?	
don't mind?	
don't really like?	
absolutely hate?	

B Make a group of four to six students. Then take turns sharing your answers. Did any of your group members choose the same clothing items?

Three Years Ago vs. Now

Reading

Read the two Internet posts. 05-07

www.jobzblogz.com

2010. 2. 23. 14:00

Hi. I'm Maria. I recently graduated from law school. I'm trying to find a job at a law firm in New York City. It's really hard to find a job. I'm supposed to go to an interview tomorrow with the law firm Miller & Stein, but I don't even have the right clothes for the interview. I'm broke because I spent all my money on law school. I can't afford to go to the department store. I'll have to borrow a jacket and skirt from my roommate. We live in the Bronx. It's a bit far from Manhattan, which is where I want to work. Even if I get this job, I'll have to commute quite far each day. Although I'll be starting at the bottom, I'm going to work hard to move up. I mean, you have to start somewhere, right?

Jman25

We've all been there Maria. Keep your head up. You'll make it to the top eventually!

Teddybear11

I went through the same thing. But now I'm a lawyer at a big firm in Manhattan. If you work hard, you can do it!

OhMaria

Thanks for the nice comments, guys. I really appreciate it. I'll do my best!

www.jobzblogz.com

2013. 10. 13. 12:10

Hey, it's me, Maria, again. Here I am outside my office. I've just become a partner at Miller & Stein. My coworkers are going to take me out to a nice restaurant in Manhattan to celebrate. It's been a hard three years, but I've learned a lot. I'm making a six-figure salary at the law firm now. My living situation has improved. I don't need a roommate any more. I can afford to live in a good-sized apartment all by myself. My wardrobe is much nicer now, too. I wear designer suits to work, and I live in Manhattan. I spend a lot of time going to bars and clubs in Manhattan with my coworkers. I have a boyfriend. He's a stockbroker on Wall Street. We are really happy together. I have a great life, so hang in there everyone. It definitely gets better!

Jman25

Hey, Maria! Long time, no see! I'm so glad you made it. Congratulations!

Teddybear11

Way to go Maria! I knew you could do it!

OhMaria

Thanks for cheering for me even while I was doubting myself. I won't doubt myself again!

*six-figure salary = a salary of $100,000 to $999,999 per year

Comprehension Check Answer the questions about the Internet posts.

1. Why was Maria worried about her job interview in 2010?
2. Where did Maria live in 2010? Where does she live now?
3. How has Maria's living situation changed?
4. How has Maria's wardrobe changed?
5. What does Maria's boyfriend do?

Group Work

A Choose one member of your group to talk about how his or her work life, style, living situation, and romantic life were three years ago and how they are now. When he or she is ready, listen and take notes.

Group Member's Name: ______________		
	Three Years Ago	**Now**
Work Life		
Style		
Living Situation		
Romantic Life		

B Write a short essay about your group member's work life, style, living situation, and romantic life three years ago and now based on the notes in the table.

Wrap-up

A Complete the conversation with the correct words from the word box.

the outlet mall	ripped off	yard sale	designer	a steal

A Where did you get this jacket? It looks expensive.

B It's a ______________ jacket, but I bought it at my neighbor's ______________ for $40.00!

A Wow! That's ______________. It's a shame that I missed it.

B No worries. You can go to ______________ with me this weekend.

A Cool. I don't mind buying items from last season. Actually, whenever I go shopping at the department store, I feel like I got ______________.

B Look at the pictures and rank the styles from 1 to 4. The style you prefer the most should be 1.

C Choose two pictures in C to compare by using the presented expressions.

casual / dressed down	classic / timeless	vintage	chic
dressed up	the latest trend	designer clothing	off-the-peg / off-the-rack

D Present an item you have with you now. Tell the class where you bought it and how much you paid for it. Once everyone has presented an item, vote to decide whose item was the best bargain.

I bought this leather bag at a flea market. It cost me $15.00. I love this bag because it looks cool. I've had it for ten years. I think it was a great bargain.

Unit 6

Immigration and Life Abroad

Warm-up

A Look at the items below and put the letters of the appropriate items in the missing parts of the pictures.

a.
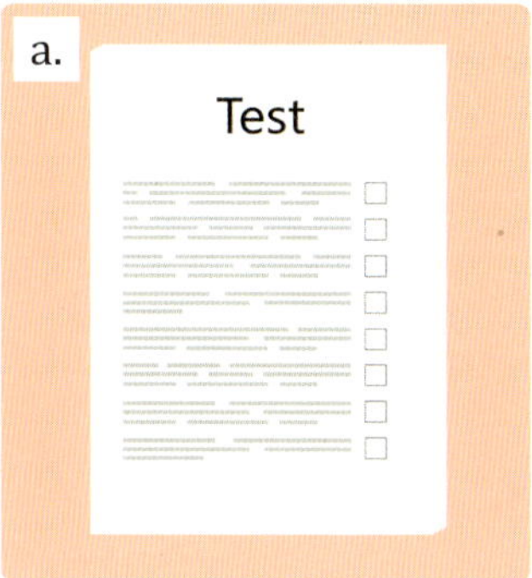

b.

c.
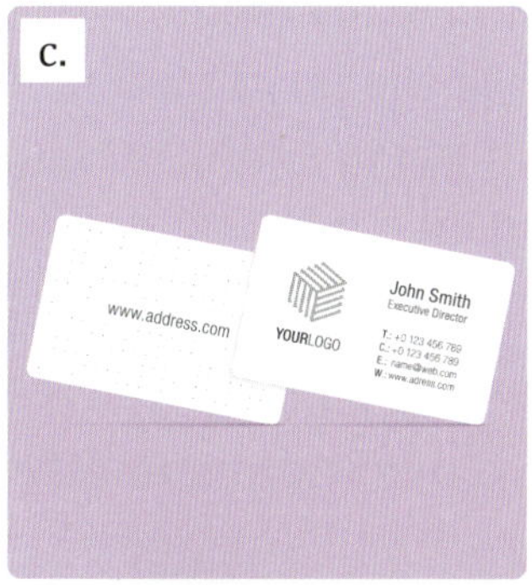

d.

B Have you ever traveled abroad? Have you ever lived abroad? If yes, answer the questions below.

1. Where did you go?
2. How long did you stay there?
3. Why did you go there?
4. Did you enjoy your time there?
5. Do you want to go abroad again?

Have you gotten your visa yet?

Conversation

Listen and practice the conversation. 06-01

A Yeonsuk, have you gotten your student visa for the U.S. yet?

B Yeah, I got it two days ago. The line at the American Embassy was really long.

A I bet. It was the same at the Australian Embassy.

B Are you going to Australia to study, Yumiko?

A No, I'm actually going on a working holiday. They have a special visa for young people who want to see the country but need to work in order to pay for the trip.

B Oh, cool! I think my cousin did something like that in Canada.

A That's funny because I had to decide between Canada and Australia. I chose Australia because the weather is nicer this time of year.

B We'll have to keep in touch during our time away.

A Yeah, for sure.

TIPS & TIPS "I bet."

"I bet." means you understand the other person's opinion or feeling about a situation.

Vocabulary

Read the sentences and then choose the letter that matches the meanings in bold.

1. You have to get **a special stamp from the immigration officer** before you enter a country.
   a. passport　　b. visa　　c. airline ticket

2. Many countries have **official buildings with offices in other countries**.
   a. embassies　　b. airports　　c. city halls

3. This is **a trip abroad where the person works in order to fund his or her trip**.
   a. study abroad program　　b. weekend getaway　　c. working holiday

4. When friends are separated from each other, they might want to **maintain contact** through email or by telephone.
   a. keep in touch　　b. get away from　　c. visit regularly

5. You can say this when **you want to show you understand a person's opinion**.
   a. Oh, cool!　　b. I bet.　　c. That's funny!

Listening

A Listen to the conversation and choose the correct answers. 06-02

1. Cassandra would like to study in Beijing for a (semester / year).
2. Cassandra has been studying Mandarin for (two / three) years.
3. Cassandra should receive a (letter of recommendation / registration form) from the professor in order to apply for the program.
4. Cassandra is especially interested in Chinese (history / cuisine).
5. Cassandra got a renewed passport last (week / month).

B Listen again and write the four additional instructions the man gives to the woman in the table.

	Get an application from the Registrar's office.
1.	
2.	
3.	
4.	

Pair Work

Going Through Customs

Complete the blanks and role-play a conversation. Take turns being the customs official and the passenger.

Customs Official	Passenger
Welcome to ______________. May I see your passport?	Here it is.
Where are you coming from?	
What is the purpose of your visit?	□ pleasure □ business □ study □ other (______________)
How long will you be staying in ______________?	□ less than a week □ about a month □ a few months □ half a year □ more than a year
Do you have anything to declare? If yes, what's the value?	□ Yes (value: $__________) □ No
Enjoy yourself!	Thank you.

I heard you got your green card.

Conversation

Listen and practice the conversation. 06-03

A Chen, is it true?

B Is what true?

A I heard that you got a green card.

B Yeah, but it's no big deal.

A No big deal? How can you say that? Now you can stay here indefinitely. My internship is almost finished, so my visa expires next month.

B Oh, I'm sorry to hear that, Yuki. My company helped me acquire a green card. I'll still be doing a lot of traveling between China and the U.S. But it's nice not to have to worry about visas any more.

A I hope to work in the U.S. and get a green card one day.

B When you graduate from university next year, send me your résumé. We're always looking for smart, hardworking young people.

Speaking | International Company vs. Domestic Company

Imagine you are Yuki and you have two job offers, one from an international company and one from your home country of Japan. Which one would you take if you were her? Look at the two options below and share your opinion with the group.

Pair Work

Working Abroad

Ask your partner the questions about living and working in another country.

1. Would you like to work in another country?
2. What do you think would be difficult about living in another country: housing, food, language, customs, etc.?
3. What are the benefits of working abroad?
4. Do you know anyone who works abroad? If yes, how often do you see him or her? How does he or she feel about working abroad?

A Would you like to work in another country?

B Sure. You only live once. The more various experiences you have, the more you can enjoy your life. I definitely want to work abroad.

Listening

A Listen to the conversation and answer the questions. 06-04

1. What does the man want to do?
   a. work in another country
   b. study abroad
   c. get a job in another city
2. What does EAD stand for?
   a. employment authorization document
   b. employing American doctors
   c. employment arrangement directors
3. What documents besides the application and the company letter does he need to submit?
   a. a copy of his birth certificate, his passport, and a social security number
   b. a copy of his birth certificate, his passport, and a copy of a photo ID
   c. a passport, a copy of a photo ID, and a social security number
4. What cannot be inferred about the man?
   a. He will try to find a job when he gets his visa.
   b. He will wait for his document to arrive.
   c. He will get a permanent work visa as well.

B Listen again and choose True or False. If it is false, change the sentence to make it true.

1. The man's company is sponsoring his visa. [True / False]
2. The embassy will use the contact information from his driver's license to contact him. [True / False]
3. The man could receive his temporary work visa in less than two months. [True / False]

Group Work

Choose a country and complete the table. You can use the Internet if you don't know the answers. Read your clues starting with the first to your group members until they can guess your chosen country.

Keep this a secret!

		Country Name: ____________
1.	Population	
2.	Size (km2)	
3.	Climate	
4.	Political System	
5.	Culture	
6.	Capital	

A The population of this country is 350 million.
B Is it India?
A No, it isn't. Do you want the second clue?
B Yes, I do.

How do you like it here?

Conversation

Listen and practice the conversation. 06-05

A How do you like working here, Ben?

B I like it a lot. But I've noticed that people in your country are expected to work really long hours.

A I know. When I worked in the United States, I was very surprised that people stopped working at 5:30 p.m.

B Really?

A Yeah. I was used to working until seven, eight, or even nine at night here. But in the U.S., my coworkers went home at five thirty on the button.

B In the U.S., we don't have to wait for our boss to go home. Workers are only expected to follow the hours in their contract.

A I like that. It's nice to be able to go home a little earlier in the evenings.

B That's for sure.

*on the button: exactly; precisely

Survey

A Survey three students in your class about their jobs. Write the answers in the table.

		Student 1	Student 2	Student 3
1.	What's your name?			
2.	When do you start work?			
3.	When do you usually finish work in the evening?			
4.	How long is your lunch break?			
5.	Do you have to work on the weekend?			
6.	How much vacation do you get in a year?			

B What time do they start and finish work on average? Who has the longest lunch break? Who works on the weekend? Who gets the least amount of vacation in a year?

Listening

A Listen to the three speakers and choose True or False. 06-06

1-2

1. Marta is still getting used to speaking English. [True / False]
2. Marta has half an hour lunch break. [True / False]

3-4

3. Shingo's family moved to the USA when he was twelve. [True / False]
4. Shingo spends most of his time at work outside. [True / False]

5-6

5. Sunny works for a large corporation in Melbourne. [True / False]
6. Sunny usually has lunch with her colleagues. [True / False]

B Listen again and complete the table.

	Marta	Shingo	Sunny
Country of origin		*Japan*	
Country working in now	*England*		*Australia*
Position at company		*technician*	
Starting time	*8:30 a.m.*		*9:00 a.m.*
Finish time		*3:30 p.m.*	
Likes	*meeting people*		
Dislikes			*missing family*

Presentation

Answer the questions about your job and present the answers to the class.

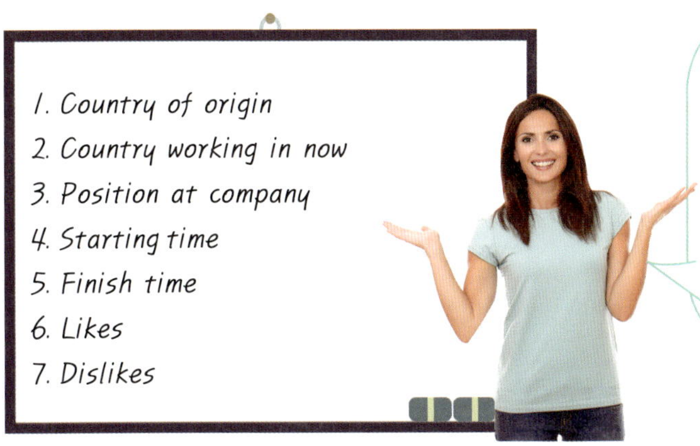

I'm Hyosun, and I'm from Seoul, Korea. I grew up in the Gangnam area of Seoul. You know, from the song *Gangnam Style*. I live in the United States now. New York City to be precise. I'm an intern at a famous fashion magazine. I start at eight in the morning and finish at eight at night...

Tips for Living Abroad

Reading

Read the website article. 06-07

www.expathandbook.com

Three Tips for Living Abroad

Writer Tara Silverstein

Everyone knows it can be very difficult to adjust to a new life overseas. After a long flight, you might find yourself in a strange land overlooking unfamiliar vistas. The cacophony of the language you don't yet understand intimidates you, and you begin to wonder if moving here was the biggest mistake of your life. Well, slow down because those of us who have relocated to foreign countries have all been there. The staff at the Expat Handbook put together the three most important tips to remember when moving to a new country, and we'd like to share them with you now, so here it goes:

1. Be open to new things! In times of stress, our first instinct is to run to the familiar. Although comforting, the familiar is not going to help us grow. We must meet new challenges head on and be willing to take risks. If you find yourself in a new country and a local person invites you to dinner, say yes! You won't know you don't like something until you try it. When I first arrived in Thailand in 2001, I was terrified of eating spicy food. And, yeah, in the early days, my mouth was on fire. But over time, I came to really appreciate spicy food. And because I was willing to put up with a little pain in the beginning of my time there, I have now experienced so many wonderful and authentic Thai dishes. Thailand has some of my favorite dishes in the world!

2. Take time to learn the language, but don't stress out about it. If you're an expat who is going to be living in a new country for a long time, it's best to learn at least some basic phrases that will allow you to communicate more clearly with the local people. Visit a bookstore in your new country. You'll probably find several beginner books that will help you learn important phrases, the names of different foods, and the number system. Go online. You'll find lots of free websites dedicated to teaching the language of the country you're in. And don't stress out. Remember that 80% of communication between humans is nonverbal. Body language, like using facial expressions or pointing, will take you far overseas.

3. Make friends with the local people. I can't imagine my life without my large group of international friends. I strongly believe that the best way to learn about a culture is to experience it with people from that culture. When I was in Thailand, I went out of my way to meet local Thai people. One of my next-door neighbors, Sansanee, became such a close friend. She was a university student and was studying English. I was a new arrival in the country and wanted to learn Thai. It was perfect. She became a great friend.

Comprehension Check Answer the questions about the article.

1. Who created the list of three tips?
2. According to the article, what do people do in times of stress?
3. Where did the author of this article mention she had lived overseas?
4. Where does the writer suggest expats find materials for learning the language?
5. How does the writer suggest expats learn about a culture?

Class Activity | Make a New Country

A Form a group of three or four people. Then create a new country. You may use parts of existing countries that you like, or you may create an entirely new one. When you are finished, present your new country to the class.

New Country's Name: ______________________	
Political System	□ democracy □ communism □ monarchy □ other (______________)
Population	□ fewer than ten million □ between twenty and ninety million □ more than a hundred million □ more than a billion □ other (______________)
Standard of Living	□ low living standards and low prices □ high living standards and high prices □ other (______________)
Climate	□ tropical □ temperate □ subarctic □ other (______________)
Food	□ rice and vegetables □ eggs, bacon, and bread □ soup and noodles □ other (______________)
Culture (music, clothes, hobbies, marriage, etc.)	
Language *You can create a name for a new language or use an existing language.*	

*monarchy: a system in which a country has a king or queen

*subarctic: a frigid climate

B Choose two groups' presentations and complete the table with information about their new countries.

	Group A	Group B
Political System		
Population		
Standard of Living		
Climate		
Food		
Culture		
Language		

C In which of the two groups' countries would you like to live? Why?

Wrap-up

A Complete the conversation with the correct words from the word box.

visa	embassy	working holiday	keep in touch

A I have some exciting news.
B What's that?
A I'm going on a ______________ to Japan.
B That's great! Have you gotten your ______________ yet?
A I went to the Japanese ______________ yesterday.
B Cool. Let's ______________ through email while you're away.
A Of course.

B Imagine you are entering Canada. Complete the conversation between a passenger and an immigration official.

A Welcome to Canada. May I see your passport?
B Sure. Here you are.
A Where are you coming from?
B ______________________________
A What is the reason for your trip?
B ______________________________
A How long do you plan on staying here?
B ______________________________
A Have you been here before?
B ______________________________
A Do you wish to declare any items?
B ______________________________

C Choose one of the sides of the argument and take notes in the table on the reasons to support your argument.

I prefer working abroad because...	I prefer working in my home country because...

D Use your notes from C in order to debate a classmate who holds the opposite opinion.

Unit 7

Dating

Warm-up

A Have you ever been on a blind date? Which picture below more accurately describes the last blind date you were on?

B Which actions below are deal breakers for you in a dating situation?

☐ Being indifferent	☐ Having bad table manners	☐ Being rude
☐ Being inconsiderate	☐ Having a bad fashion sense	☐ Having a poor sense of humor
☐ Having poor listening skills	☐ Being stingy	☐ Using inappropriate language

A Blind Date

Conversation

Listen and practice the conversation. 07-01

A Hi. Are you William?
B Yes. Are you Sarah?
A Yes. It's nice to meet you.
B It's nice to meet you, too.
A Have you been waiting long?
B No, not long. I got here about ten minutes ago. I ordered us two glasses of wine. I hope you don't mind.
A Actually, I don't drink. I mentioned it on my **dating profile**.
B Oh, no. I didn't notice that. I'm sorry. Would you like to order something else?
A Sure. I'd like a **sparkling water**.
B Okay. When the waiter comes back, I'll change the drink order. I was thinking we could order crab cakes as **starters**, lobster for the **main course**, and tiramisu for **dessert**!
A Crab cakes? Lobster? I'm a **vegetarian**.
B Oh... I think there's been a mix-up. Are you Sarah Rogers?
A No. I'm Sarah Rogan.

Vocabulary

Write the words in bold from the conversation above in the spaces under the correct pictures.

1.

2.

3.

4.

5.

6.

Listening

A Listen to the two speakers and answer the questions. 07-02

1-2

1. What does Raoul do?
   a. He's a teacher.
   b. He's a matchmaker.
   c. He's a businessman.
2. What is NOT true about Raoul?
   a. He has a seven-year-old daughter.
   b. He doesn't drink much but enjoys drinking a little beer.
   c. He got divorced 2 years ago.

3-4

3. How long has Jessica's friend Christa been dating her boyfriend?
   a. one year
   b. two years
   c. three years
4. What is true about Jessica?
   a. She was married but is now divorced.
   b. She was engaged but never married.
   c. She was engaged and has married.

B Listen again and complete Raoul's and Jessica's information on the dating profiles.

Raoul		Jessica
	Age	
MBA	Education	
	Marital Status	*single*
Yes	Children	
skiing & tennis	Likes	
	Dislikes	*TV*

Pair Work Imagine you are running a blind dating service and your partner is your customer. Ask your partner the questions on the questionnaire and write your partner's answers on the form.

Mr. / Ms. ________		
	Age	
	Body Type	□ thin □ slim □ medium build □ curvy □ chubby □ overweight □ athletic & muscular □ other (________)
	Education	□ high school diploma □ bachelor's degree □ master's degree □ doctor's degree □ other (________)
Marital Status	□ single □ separated □ divorced □ other (________)	
Children	□ Yes □ No	
Interests	□ music □ movies □ artwork □ reading □ sports □ fashion □ festivals □ animals □ volunteering □ travel □ online games □ drawing □ fishing □ other (________)	
Smoking / Drinking	□ none □ smoking □ drinking □ both	
Special Notes		

A How old are you?
B I'm 26 years old.
A How would you describe your body type?
B I work out a lot. I think I'm athletic and muscular.

We're both in love.

Conversation

Listen and practice the conversation. 07-03

A How are things going with you and Patrick, Brianna?
B We're doing really well.
A Is it official yet?
B Official?
A Yeah. Are you boyfriend and girlfriend now?
B Yes. We've been exclusive for a couple of months now.
A Do you think he's the one?
B We haven't really talked seriously about marriage yet. But we're both in love.
A That's great. I'm so happy for you.
B Thank you. Patrick's such a great guy. I can't wait for you to meet him this weekend.
A I can't wait either.

Vocabulary | Interesting Jobs

Look at the pictures and read the sentences. Then write the appropriate expressions in the correct places.

break up with flirting with turnoff crush turn-on love at first sight

1. 

Chris keeps ______________ Sookie. Yesterday, I saw them at a café, and he was stroking her hair and touching her cheek.

2. 

I can't concentrate on my biology class. I just can't stop looking at Tom. To be honest, I think I have a big ______________ on him.

3. 

I think I have to ______________ my girlfriend. I'm afraid to say it, but I'm not satisfied with the relationship anymore.

4. 

I really like my boyfriend. But there's one thing I can't stand. He sometimes picks his nose. It's such a ______________.

5. 

Joe bumped into Kelly on the street and instinctively knew she was the one. It was ______________.

6. 

He opened the door for me and pulled out my chair at dinner. His gentlemanly behavior was a real ______________ for me!

Listening

A Listen to the dating dos and don'ts and turn the five false statements into true statements. 07-04

1. Dating in the digital era is similar to the pre-Internet era.
2. People rarely remember a first meeting.
3. Choose an informal place like a fast-food restaurant.
4. Discuss topics like religion and politics.
5. Don't let the man pay.

B According to the talk, what are the woman's dating dos and don'ts? Fill in the blanks.

Dating Dos and Don'ts

- Do make a good first ______________.
- Do meet in a place that's ______________... not too formal / not too basic.
- Don't be shy.
- Do be a good ______________.
- Don't talk about your ______________.
- Don't stare at your smartphone the whole time.

Group Work

Your First Date

A Make a group of three students. Write your answers and your group members' answers to the questions about your first dates in the table.

	Student 1 (me)	Student 2	Student 3
Where did you go?			
What did you do?			
Who paid?			
How was the date?			
Did you go out again?			

B Discuss who had the most interesting first date. Choose a group representative and present your group member's story to the class.

Jamal went on his first date when he was fifteen years old. He went to an amusement park with a girl from his high school. Jamal paid five dollars to play a game where he could win a prize for his date. He just had to pop three balloons using three darts. Unfortunately, he...

She dumped me.

Conversation

Listen and practice the conversation. 07-05

A What happened, Nate?

B Tina called me and said she needed to talk. We decided to meet at a coffee shop near my apartment.

A And then what happened?

B Well, she was acting really strangely.

A What do you mean?

B She wouldn't make eye contact with me. So I asked her what was wrong.

A What did she say?

B She said she wasn't happy in the relationship anymore.

A Oh, no.

B And then she dumped me.

A I'm really sorry, Nate. Let me buy you another glass of wine.

B Okay. Thanks.

Grammar

A Let's learn about reported speech.

Direct Speech	→	Reported Speech
She **is** not happy.	present simple → past simple	She said (that) she **was** not happy.
We **are having** a good time in Florida.	present continuous → past continuous	My parents said (that) they **were having** a good time in Florida.
I **saw** a bear in the forest.	past simple → past perfect	John said (that) he **had seen** a bear in the forest.
We **have been** to Mexico three times.	present perfect → past perfect	They said (that) they **had been** to Mexico three times.
I **had eaten** at that restaurant.	past perfect → past perfect	Lina said (that) she **had eaten** at that restaurant.

B Change the examples of direct speech into reported speech.

1. Sam: "I saw a car accident on my way to work today."
2. my parents: "We are meeting the Millers at 7:00 p.m. on Tuesday."
3. Dr. Kristine: "I am pleased with your presentation."
4. Chen: "I have played tennis with her many times."

Listening

A Listen to the two related conversations and answer the questions. 07-06

1. Where did Charles say he had gone in the afternoon?
   a. He said he had gone to the restaurant.
   b. He said he had gone to the gym.
   c. He said he had gone to the jewelry store.
2. Where did Kathy find the receipt?
   a. She found it in Charles's bag.
   b. She found it in Charles's pants pocket.
   c. She found it in Charles's wallet.
3. What favor does Charles ask of Bill and Janelle?
   a. He asks them to babysit his children.
   b. He asks them to lend him $5,000.
   c. He asks them to celebrate Kathy's birthday.
4. What kind of present is Charles going to give Kathy for her birthday?
   a. a gold watch
   b. diamond earrings
   c. a diamond bracelet
5. When is Kathy's birthday?
   a. tomorrow
   b. next week
   c. next month

B Listen to the conversation between Janelle and Bill and discuss the question with your classmates.

What do you think Bill and Janelle should do? Should they tell Kathy and ruin the surprise, or should they remain silent and let Kathy continue to be angry?

Dating and Technology

Reading

A Read the article. 07-07

The Wisconsin Times
: Lifestyle

April 15th

Dating in the Digital Age

Francine Waterston | Writer

Dating has changed a lot in the past two decades. Before the advent of smartphone technology, men typically had to approach women to ask them out. For some men, it took time to work up the courage to approach women, and for others, asking them out came easily. Some women even took the initiative to ask men out. Regardless of the ease with which one asks out another, all of these examples have one thing in common: face-to-face contact. When our generation was young, we had to look people in the eyes and have a conversation. It wasn't easy, but it was character building.

In the digital age, dating is quite different. You no longer need to muster up the courage to approach someone. You can just send a text message. Single people find it less threatening to send a vague text message like this: "You busy tomorrow?" And the people receiving the message find it much easier to reject any unwanted invitations by replying with a message like this: "Sorry, big test tomorrow!☹" Modern single people favor this method because neither party has to deal with the pain of being rejected or the discomfort of rejecting someone. But is this a good trend?

According to Dr. Robert Lawler, a behavioral psychologist and author of *Swipe Right: Dating in the Digital Age*, we are in a transitional moment. The dating norms of the past no longer apply, and a new type of behavior is emerging. He says it is true that technology can protect us from rejection, but that isn't necessarily a good thing. Rejection reminds us that we are human, and it allows us to grow and to become better people. He says the worst thing we can do is cut ourselves off completely from the outside world. Face-to-face contact with friends and romantic partners is a very important part of life, and no technology can replace that.

Comprehension Check Answer the questions about the article.

1. How did people ask each other out on dates before smartphone technology?
2. How do people ask each other out now?
3. Why do young people prefer to ask out others by using text messages?
4. What kind of moment does Dr. Lawler believe we are in?
5. What does Dr. Lawler think about rejection?

B What method do you prefer to use when asking someone out on a date?

Questionnaire

A Exchange books with a partner and let him or her complete the dating questionnaire.

	Questioner: ________________ **Respondent:** ________________
Are you a romantic person?	□ Yes □ No
What's your type?	□ stylish □ smart □ kind □ chic □ tidy □ humble □ sociable □ confident □ cool □ hip □ reserved □ thoughtful □ talkative □ bold □ hilarious □ clumsy □ calm □ conservative □ liberal □ other (________________)
Where is a good place to meet people?	□ restaurant □ café □ pub □ park □ grocery store □ club □ office □ dating app □ college / university □ other (________________)
Where is a good place to go on a first date?	□ restaurant □ café □ pub □ park □ museum □ movie theater □ concert □ club □ amusement park □ other (________________)
Who do you think should pay on a date?	□ man □ woman □ go Dutch
Have you been on a blind date before?	□ Yes □ No
• If yes, how would you grade it?	0 terrible — 50 so-so — 100 perfect
• If no, would you like to go on a blind date?	□ Yes □ No

B Get your book back from your partner and write about your partner by using the answers from the questionnaire.

C Make a presentation about your partner to the class.

My partner thinks he is a romantic person. He prefers a woman who is stylish, smart, and chic. He thinks pubs are good places to meet people and good places to go on dates. You can talk together and get to know a person in a pub. He thinks the man should pay for the first date. He's never been on a blind date, but he'd be willing to try it.

Wrap-up

A Change the examples of direct speech into reported speech.

ex. "I like online dating." (I = Rita) *Rita said she liked online dating.*

1. "I am watching the baseball game." (I = Simon)
2. "We have been to Paris." (We = Yoon and Ganghyeok)
3. "I went on a date with Brian last weekend." (I = Ella)
4. "We are going to stay in Finland before going to South Korea." (We = Effie and Tony)

B Fill in the blanks with the correct words in the word box.

crush	flirting with	broke up	love at first sight	turnoff

1. April knew she loved Jacob the first time she saw him. It was ______________ for her.
2. My roommate was really depressed after he ______________ with his girlfriend.
3. Subin has a huge ______________ on the lead singer of the K-pop group B.O.Y.
4. Steven is ______________ Elena, but she doesn't seem interested.
5. Bad manners is a real ______________ for most men and women.

C Conduct a short survey about blind dating and use the data from your survey to give a short presentation about blind dating.

Question 1. Have you ever been on a blind date?
Question 2. If yes, how was it?

Three of the students in my survey have been on blind dates. But two of them had bad experiences. One student met her boyfriend on a blind date...

D Talk about how your parents or grandparents met.

Unit
8 Traffic

Warm-up

A Look at the pictures and say what happened in each situation.

B Have you experienced any of these situations firsthand? If yes, what happened?

There must have been an accident.

Conversation

Listen and practice the conversation. 08-01

A We haven't moved an inch in ten minutes!
B The traffic is terrible. Should we change lanes?
A It's bumper to bumper in every lane.
B Can we take another route?
A I don't think so. The next exit is several kilometers away.
B What should we do?
A We'll just have to wait.
B Why do you think there's gridlock?
A There must have been an accident up ahead.
B Oh, dear! I hear ambulance sirens.
A I hear them, too. Gosh, I hope it isn't bad.
B Me, too.

Vocabulary

Look at the pictures and read the sentences. Then fill in the blanks with the words from the word box.

bumper to bumper	route	sirens	pedestrians	residential	fine

1.

A police camera caught me driving 90km per hour in an 80km per hour zone. Now I have to pay a ______________.

2.

Alex decided to take a new ______________ to work this morning, so he arrived ten minutes early.

3.

Police ______________ contribute to noise pollution in big cities, but they are necessary for keeping people safe.

4.

The news reported that two ______________ were injured in a traffic accident last night.

5.

The traffic is always ______________ during rush hour.

6.

The speed limit in ______________ areas is 30km per hour.

Listening

A Listen to the man talking about his job as a traffic signal coordinator. Then answer the questions. 08-02

1. Which of the following describes Ian's job correctly?
   a. He finds cars that have broken traffic rules.
   b. He assists computers by sending the correct information to the Road Traffic Authority.
   c. He analyzes information from smart machines and controls the traffic.
2. What is Ian's duty as a traffic signal coordinator?
   a. to ensure people cross the street safely
   b. to ensure that traffic moves smoothly
   c. to ensure that rush hour time periods are reduced
3. What should Ian do if there's a traffic accident?
   a. open road where the accident occurred
   b. close the roads until the area is secure
   c. open an alternate route for drivers
4. According to the talk, what does Ian use to coordinate traffic?
   a. maps, charts, books, and computers
   b. apps, computer software, and graphs
   c. maps, charts, graphs, and computers

B Listen again and choose True or False.

1. Ian Bloom works for the city of Milwaukee, Wisconsin. [True / False]
2. Most people know city traffic is coordinated by people. [True / False]
3. Ian has a team of four people. [True / False]
4. Part of Ian's job is to ensure people get to and from work safely. [True / False]

Pair Work Ask your partner the questions on the traffic congestion questionnaire.

Traffic Congestion Questionnaire	
How long is your daily commute (to and from school or work)?	□ less than 1 hour □ 1-2 hours □ 2-3 hours □ more than 3 hours □ I don't commute by road.
How often are you stuck in traffic jams?	□ daily □ weekly □ monthly □ rarely □ never
Do you have a car?	□ Yes □ No
If yes, do you use a navigation system in your car?	□ Yes □ No
Do you use your navigation system to avoid traffic jams?	□ Yes □ No
What is the most annoying thing about being stuck in a traffic jam? Please rank each statement from 1 to 5 with 1 being what you find the most annoying.	( ) wasting too much time ( ) boredom ( ) not knowing why there is a traffic jam ( ) discomfort from sitting too long, back pain, needing to use the restroom ( ) nothing good to listen to on the radio

A How long is your daily commute?
B It takes almost a half an hour.

I see a free space right there!

Conversation

Listen and practice the conversation. 08-03

A Hmm, where should we park?
B How about the parking ramp?
A The ramp is $10 an hour. Let's look for something on the street.
B Okay, but it's going to be tough to find a spot.
A Don't worry about it. There are lots of spaces on the street.
B I'm not so sure about that.

(30 minutes later)

A I can't believe there isn't a single spot open on the street!
B Can we just park in the ramp now? The game is about to start.
A Oh, there's a free parking space right there!
B That's a disabled parking space. The fine for parking there is $300.
A Okay, let's park in the ramp.

Vocabulary | Traffic Violations

A Match the traffic violations to the correct pictures.

speeding illegal parking getting pulled over running a red light
texting while driving jaywalking car vandalism drunk driving

1.

2.

3.

4.

5.

6.

7.

8.

B Have you ever seen someone committing a traffic violation? If yes, check the ones you have seen.

Listening

Listen to the conversations and answer the questions. 08-04

1-2

1. What was the woman doing while driving?
   a. She was using her navigation system.
   b. She was sending a text message.
   c. She was drinking coffee.

2. What was the woman supposed to do?
   a. She was supposed to slow down.
   b. She was not supposed to use her smartphone.
   c. She was supposed to attach her smartphone to the dashboard.

3-4

3. Why did the man get pulled over?
   a. He ran a red light.
   b. He ran a stop sign.
   c. He was speeding.

4. Why is the police officer sure the man committed a traffic offence?
   a. She recorded the incident on a police car camera.
   b. Another driver saw him commit the traffic offence.
   c. She took a picture of the incident with her smartphone.

TIPS & TIPS cars vs. bicycles, motorcycles, and motorbikes

If you are driving a car, you are the **driver**.
If you are riding in a car, but you are not driving, you are a **passenger**.
If you are riding a bicycle, you are a **cyclist**.
If you are riding a motorcycle or a motorbike, you are a **biker** or a **motorcyclist**.
In English, we **ride** a bicycle, motorcycle, or motorbike, and we **drive** a car.

Writing a Police Report

Read the paragraph and complete the report.

At 5:30 p.m. on Halloween last year, an accident occurred at the intersection of Elk Drive and Riverside Place. A tan four-door sedan ran a red light and hit a cyclist who was crossing the street. The cyclist was knocked off of the bicycle but sustained no serious injuries. His bicycle, however, was damaged beyond repair. The sedan also sustained some damage. The front bumper was scratched, and the right headlight was cracked. Officer Gary Pittman was the first officer to arrive at the scene of the accident. He interviewed the driver and the cyclist and determined that the driver was at fault. The driver was ticketed and fined for running a red light. The driver was also asked to replace the bicycle he damaged in the accident. The driver agreed to buy the cyclist a new bicycle.

POLICE REPORT

Date ____________

Time ____________

Place of Incident ____________

Details of Event ____________

Actions Taken ____________

I got a flat tire.

Conversation

Listen and practice the conversation. 08-05

A Hello?
B Hey, Bonnie. It's Nigel.
A Where are you? My parents and I are waiting.
B I got a flat tire. I called for some emergency roadside assistance. They're sending someone as soon as possible.
A Our dinner reservations are at seven o'clock. What should we do?
B Why don't I meet you at the restaurant? It shouldn't take that long.
A Can't you fix the flat tire yourself?
B I'm wearing my best suit. I don't want to ruin it.
A Okay. I understand. You need to make a good first impression with my parents, and we're off to a bad start.
B Don't worry. As soon as he changes the tire, I'll go straight to the restaurant. I'll only be 20 minutes late.
A Okay. See you soon.

Useful Expressions

A Write the letters of the appropriate statements in the correct boxes.

a. My car won't start. I think the engine's dead.
b. My car is being towed.
c. I got a flat tire.
d. My car got dented.
e. I ran out of gas.
f. I got stopped by the police.

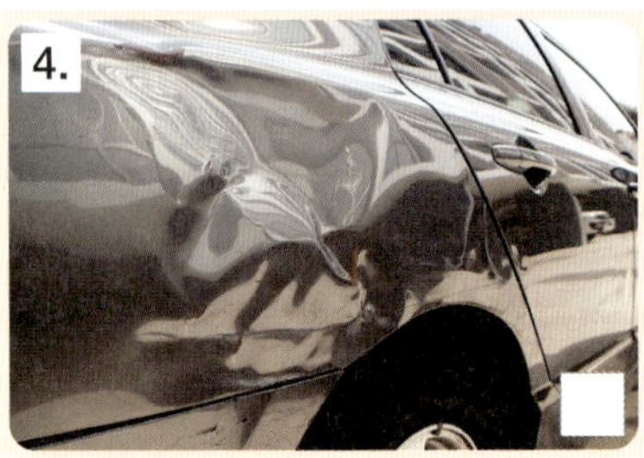

B Say what you think the drivers should do in these situations.

If you get a flat tire, you should change it yourself.

Listening

A Listen to the conversation and choose the correct answers. 08-06

1. The man prefers the (station wagon / van).
2. The man and the woman have (a child/ children).
3. The van is (roomier / less roomy) than the station wagon.
4. The woman prefers the (station wagon / van).
5. The couple will buy the (station wagon / van).

B Listen again and complete the information in the advertisements.

◊ Car Type ______________________

◊ Year ______________________

◊ Price ______________________

◊ Kilometers ______________________

◊ Car Type ______________________

◊ Year ______________________

◊ Price ______________________

◊ Kilometers ______________________

Pair Work

Imagine you and your partner have $20,000 to spend on a car, but you don't have to spend it all. Which car would you buy?

2006 Jupiter
Price $3,500
Kilometers 120,000

2012 Racer
Price $13,000
Kilometers 80,000

2014 Arizona
Price $18,000
Kilometers 35,000

2013 Renegade
Price $15,000
Kilometers 50,000

A I think we should buy the 2006 Jupiter. It's only $3,500, so we can use the extra money to purchase something more important than a car.

B I disagree. The Jupiter is more than ten years old and has too many kilometers on it. It's going to break down and cost a lot of money to fix. I think we should buy the Renegade.

The Car of the Future

Reading

A Read the letter. 08-07

Car Tech Monthly Magazine — October

Letters from the Editors

The Car of the Future

Dear *Car Tech Monthly Magazine* Readers:

One of the most common questions readers of *Car Tech Monthly Magazine* ask our editors is what the car of the future will be like. We decided to do a little research and found some interesting facts about cars of the not-so-distant future and beyond. Here are the three most interesting ones we found:

1. Within the next five years, most, if not all, new cars will come equipped with Internet connectivity. Most mid-level and luxury brands will function as their own Internet hotspots. Cloud playlists will be available simply by using voice command, and perhaps the obsolete CD player and radio will find themselves on the factory floor, unnecessary artifacts from the days of old.
2. Within the next ten years, many drivers may quite literally be asleep at the wheel. That's right. Self-driving cars are the future. In fact, self-driving cars are already on the roads. Tesla Motors drivers have the option of controlling the vehicle manually or allowing the automated self-driving technology to kick-in and take over driving duties. Although a very small segment of the driving community can afford a self-driving car now, prices are expected to decrease rapidly as more versions of cars with self-driving technology become available on the market.
3. By 2030, more than half of new cars produced are expected to be electric cars. There are a number of reasons for this, climate change being one of the most important. Some of the world's largest cities are choking on horrible smog related to car pollution, and by switching to electric cars, they will be able to eliminate a large portion of that air pollution.

We'll be back next month to answer all of your tech questions. Thanks!

Car Tech Monthly Editors

Comprehension Check Answer the questions about the letter.

1. What does the article say about cars built within the next five years?
2. What could happen to radios and CD players in cars?
3. What does the article say about cars built within the next ten years?
4. Why are some large cities in the world switching to electric cars?

B What do you find exciting about cars of the future?

Writing

Think about your dream car. Go online and fill in the blanks with information about your dream car. Then write a short essay about your dream car.

Car Name

Origin	□ domestic □ foreign
Brand	
Type	□ economy □ SUV □ sedan □ sports □ luxury
Color	□ black □ white □ silver □ navy □ red □ other (________________)
Price	□ \$20,000 - \$50,000 □ \$50,000 - \$100,000 □ \$100,000+
Mileage	
Options	

Wrap-up

A Use a dictionary to write the definitions of the words.

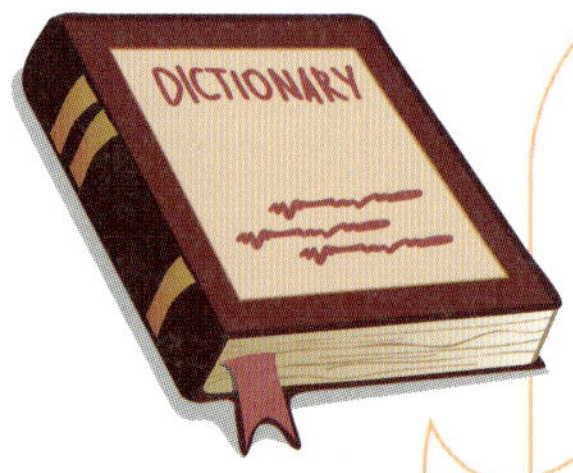

1. bumper-to-bumper

2. route

3. fine

4. pedestrian

5. residential

6. siren

7. get pulled over

8. jaywalking

B Write three examples of traffic offences in the table. Then say what the penalty for each offence is in your country.

	Traffic Offence	Penalty
	Speeding	*If you drive 80km per hour in a 60km per hour zone, you have to pay a $50.00 fine.*
1.		
2.		
3.		

C Say what happened to the people in each situation.

D Talk about your first car. If you have not owned a car, what kind of car would you like to buy as a first car?

Unit
9
The Environment and Volunteer Work

Warm-up

A What are the people in the pictures doing? Check the activities you have participated in before or would like to participate in in the future.

B Ask your partner which type of volunteering seems the most worthwhile and the reasons he or she thinks so.

We reuse one-sided copies.

Conversation

Listen and practice the conversation. 09-01

A Jim, can I talk to you for a moment?
B Sure, Fiona. What's up?
A I've noticed that you have been putting the weekly reports in the recycling bin.
B Yes, that's right.
A We try not to recycle one-sided copies until both sides are used.
B I'm sorry. I didn't know that.
A Don't worry about it. You're new.
B What should I do with one-sided copies?
A Put them in this bin next to the printer. We use the blank side for interoffice memoranda.
B Okay.
A But don't use this paper if you're sending a document to a client.
B Of course not.
A And if a document is confidential, then you should use the paper shredder.
B Okay, got it, Fiona. Thanks.

Vocabulary

Match the words to the correct pictures.

recycling bins compost paper shredder reusable
energy efficient aluminum trash bag waste

1.

2.

3.

4.

5.

6.

7.

8.

Listening

A Listen to the talk and answer the questions. 09-02

1. What is true about the breakroom in Vanessa's office?
   a. There are not enough trash bins.
   b. There is a small trash bin.
   c. There are too many trash bins.

2. What is Vanessa afraid of regarding the waste in her office?
   a. She's afraid the garbage in the office will get mixed up with the recyclables.
   b. She's afraid that the recyclable waste will end up in a landfill with the regular trash.
   c. She's worried that the nonrecyclable trash will be recycled by the cleaning staff.

3. Why doesn't Vanessa want to tell the problem to her coworkers?
   a. She's worried it will offend them.
   b. She's worried they might tell the boss.
   c. She's worried they will give her more work.

4. What can be inferred about Vanessa?
   a. She is the only one that recycles at her workplace.
   b. She uploaded her video before.
   c. She will not respond to comments made by her viewers.

B Read the comments section. Whose suggestion do you agree with? Who do you think Vanessa will agree with?

Jerkyboy44

Hey, Vanessa. I think you should just forget about it. It's probably too late to save the Earth. Just live for now and don't think about the future.

Funnygirl89

Don't listen to Jerkyboy44. He doesn't know what he's talking about. We need to protect the Earth. I'm a little shy like you, and I don't like to cause problems at work. Maybe you could wait until they take out the trash at the end of the day. Then, you could separate all the cans and bottles yourself. It will take time, but at least you will be helping the environment.

Earthangel

I definitely agree with funnygirl89 about not listening to jerkyboy44. He's just wrong. But I also think that separating the bottles and cans by yourself will take forever. At my place of work, we have four trash bins, each a different color. We throw cans in the red one, bottles and plastic in the blue one, paper in the yellow one, and regular trash in the black one. It's as simple as purchasing three more trash bins. Ask your office manager if there's money in the budget for that. I'm sure she'd be happy to help the environment. Cya!

C Listen to Vanessa's reply. Then summarize what she says by filling in the blanks.

Summary: Vanessa ____________ because the workers in her office ____________________. She made a YouBlog video about her problem. In the video, she asked for ____________ to the problem. One commenter, named ______________, gave her ___________________, and now the problem in her office ___________________.

I hate that car alarm!

Conversation

Listen and practice the conversation. 09-03

A Are you sleeping?

B Huh?

A How can you sleep right now? That car alarm is going off again. It's 3:00 a.m.!

B Oh, I guess it doesn't really bother me.

A It bothers me a lot. I hate that car alarm!

B What do you want me to do?

A I don't know.

B Do you know whose car it is?

A No.

(5 minutes later)

B There you go. It's off now, so you can go back to sleep.

A But I'm wide awake now.

Vocabulary | Types of Pollution

Look at the pictures and complete the definitions by filling in the blanks with the words in the box. Then match them to the correct types of pollution.

mutative chemicals atmosphere radioactive contamination nutrients

1.  the ___________ of bodies of water such as lakes, rivers, and oceans •
2.  removing the important ___________ through the use of pesticides and other toxic ___________ •
3.  the poisoning of the ___________ by harmful substances •
4.  causing dangerous ___________ diseases by releasing ___________ material •

• a. radioactive pollution

• b. water pollution

• c. soil pollution

• d. air pollution

Listening

A Listen to the conversation and answer the questions. 09-04

1. What magazine is Maria reading?
   a. *Health and Fitness Magazine*
   b. *Happy Lifestyle Magazine*
   c. *Healthy Lifestyle Magazine*

2. What does the circadian rhythm do?
   a. It prevents us from waking up early in the morning.
   b. It balances the amount of light our eyes receive.
   c. It regulates our bodies' sleep patterns.

3. What is NOT true about light pollution?
   a. It prevents natural light from repairing our cells.
   b. It can lead to insomnia.
   c. It is caused by TV and smartphones.

4. What does light pollution do?
   a. It wakes us up in the middle of the night.
   b. It fools our bodies into thinking night is day.
   c. It tricks our bodies into thinking it's always nighttime.

5. Why is poor sleep dangerous to your health?
   a. It results in faster cellular repair.
   b. It results in more damage to your cells.
   c. It results in the loss of appetite.

6. What can someone do to avoid light pollution?
   a. You can install thick curtains in your bedroom and avoid using your phone before bed.
   b. You can put thick curtains in your bedroom and use your phone before bed.
   c. You can avoid using your phone before bed and install thin curtains.

B Listen again and choose True or False.

1. Maria is reading an article about health and noise pollution. [True / False]
2. The circadian rhythm is important for maintaining our sleep cycle. [True / False]
3. Cell damage is a positive result of light pollution. [True / False]
4. Our bodies repair cell damage during the day. [True / False]

Presentation

A Make a group of three students. Choose either noise pollution or light pollution and write one complete sentence describing each item below. You can use the Internet.

1. Definition: ____________________
2. Characteristic: ____________________
3. Example: ____________________
4. Solution: ____________________

B Choose a group representative and give a presentation using the sentences above.

We're going to clean up a park.

Conversation

Listen and practice the conversation. 09-05

A Scott, are you going to volunteer on Saturday?

B Volunteer for what?

A We're cleaning up Griffin Park on Saturday. Didn't you get the email?

B I haven't checked my inbox yet. What's it about?

A The volunteer committee decided it would be a good idea to clean up a local park. We're going to provide garbage bags and trash pickers. Then, the volunteers will pick up the trash.

B I took my kids to Griffin Park last weekend, and I was shocked by how dirty it was.

A The city's budget cuts have left the park in poor condition. It's really sad.

B I would love to participate in the cleanup effort. How do I sign up?

A Just reply to the email and let the committee know you're going.

Pair Work Ask your partner the questions in the questionnaire and check the appropriate boxes.

1.	Have you ever volunteered?	□ Yes □ No
2.	If yes, what kind of volunteering did you do?	□ disaster relief / cleanup □ environmental conservation □ urban cleanup □ anti-war protesting □ food / money donation □ education □ animal protection □ other ( )
3.	Does your company or school volunteer in your city?	□ Yes □ No
4.	If yes, what kind of volunteer work does it do?	□ disaster relief / cleanup □ environmental conservation □ urban cleanup □ anti-war protesting □ food / money donation □ education □ animal protection □ other ( )
5.	Are there any volunteer organizations in your country?	□ Yes □ No
6.	If yes, what kinds of volunteering do people do in the organizations?	□ disaster relief / cleanup □ environmental conservation □ urban cleanup □ anti-war protesting □ food / money donation □ education □ animal protection □ other ( )
7.	What benefits do you get from volunteering?	□ feeling of making a difference □ personal growth □ creating a better world □ other ( )

A Have you ever volunteered?

B Yes, I have. I took an abandoned dog from my local shelter for a walk.

Listening

A Listen to the talk and change the false statements into true statements. 09-06

1. The company is going to dedicate the next eight weeks to the project.
2. The city has a budget surplus.
3. Volunteers cannot bring their own tools to the project.
4. The company will pay for table tennis and video games.
5. Prizes will be given to all of the volunteers.

B Listen again and complete the table.

InfoTech Volunteer Project	
Type of Project	
Number of Volunteers	
Location	
Budget	
Starting Date	
Finish Date	

Group Work

Project Proposal

A Make a group of four or five students and create a proposal for a volunteer project in your city by completing the form.

Volunteer Project	
Type of Project	
Number of Volunteers	
Location	
Budget	
Starting Date	
Finish Date	

B Share the complete proposal with the class.

Voluntourism

Reading

A Read the article. 09-07

Make a Difference Travel Company

Are you an adventurous person who also cares about people and wants to make a difference? Then maybe voluntourism is the right kind of travel experience for you. Voluntourism is the decision to turn your vacation into an opportunity to help disadvantaged people and to experience a new country and a new culture at the same time. Here at MDTA, our goal is to find the right opportunity for you. We want you to visit and explore a country you have always dreamed of visiting, but we also want to integrate meaningful volunteer work into your voluntrip.

When planning your trip, you get to decide what kind of volunteer work you want to do. We also want to know what your special skill sets are, so we can match those skill sets to projects that require your expertise. For example, we have had architects, plumbers, electricians, and construction workers participate in our overseas trips. In those cases, we matched our travelers to projects in foreign countries that needed new buildings built such as schools, churches, and community centers. Our volunteers' experience in the fields of design and construction was desperately needed and helped the projects immensely.

But it's not all work and no play. We also want our volunteers to experience the culture. At night, our project leaders take you into the cities so you can experience the country's cuisine, nightlife, and people. By working together and doing something positive for the community, you will be surprised by how quickly amazing friendships with the local people are formed. Almost all of our volunteers cite their volunteer work overseas as one of the most enriching experiences of their lives. If you want to make a difference by taking a volunteer vacation overseas, contact us at (1) 393-3939. Our operators are standing by. You can make an appointment with one of our voluntravel agents. Who knows? You might find yourself doing great work in another country in no time!

Comprehension Check Answer the questions about the article.

1. What is voluntourism?
2. Who decides what kind of volunteer work you do?
3. What examples does the article cite with regard to the types of jobs former volunteers had?
4. Who introduces the volunteers to the city?
5. What do the voluntravel agents do?

B Do you think you would be interested in voluntourism? Why or why not?

Role-play

A Imagine you work for the Make a Difference Travel Agency and your partner is interested in voluntourism. Interview your partner, so you can arrange a trip for your partner.

1. Name

2. Age

3. Email Address

4. Job / Skills

5. Language

6. Personality

7. Traveling alone / with Others

8. Special Requests

B Write an email to your partner proposing a trip by using the answers in the interview. Tell your partner which country he or she will travel to and the kind of volunteer work your partner will be doing there.

To: *Your partner's email address*

Travel Plan from MDTA

From: *Your email address*

Dear *Your partner's name*,

____

____

____

Sincerely,

Your name

C Exchange textbooks with your partner. Reply to his or her email by accepting or declining the trip proposal from MDTA.

To: *Your partner's email address*

Re: Travel Plan from MDTA

From: *Your email address*

Dear *Your partner's name*,

____

____

____

Sincerely,

Your name

Wrap-up

A Read the definitions and fill in the blanks with the words in the box.

waste	compost	reusable	trash bag
energy efficient	recycling bins	aluminum	paper shredder

1. ______________ : Most cans, especially soda cans, are made of this material.
2. ______________ : another word for garbage or trash
3. ______________ : a machine that disposes of confidential documents by cutting them into small strips
4. ______________ : not wasting energy; using a small amount of energy
5. ______________ : containers that are used to separate recyclable material such as plastic, cans, bottles, and paper
6. ______________ : a mixture of decayed plants and vegetable waste which is added to the soil to help plants grow
7. ______________ : things that can be used more than once
8. ______________ : a plastic bag that holds waste

B Say what kind of volunteer work you would like to do in your city. Share your answer with a partner.

I would like to work with children in my city. I want to tutor them in difficult subjects like math and science.

I want to build houses for underprivileged people. I like to work with my hands.

C Find out what type of pollution is the biggest problem in your city or country.

D Write a short essay about how to prevent or decrease the type of the pollution you mentioned in C.

Unit 10 Fine Arts

Warm-up

Look at the pictures. Write the words from the box in the spaces under the correct pictures.

colorful	threatening	comfortable	gloomy	pleasant
miserable	peaceful	depressing	romantic	anxious

1.

Two Women on the Shore, 1898
Edvard Munch (1863-1944)

- *dark*
- *uneasy*
-
-
-
-
-

2.

Picking Flowers, 1875
Renoir, Pierre Auguste (1841-1919)

- *bright*
- *relaxing*
-
-
-
-
-

This is amazing!

Conversation

Listen and practice the conversation. 10-01

A Wow! This place is so big.
B I know. I can't believe it. Where should we start?
A My travel book suggests we start at Egyptian antiquities.
B It does?
A Yes, because it's near the Louvre entrance. Then, we can move on to Hellenistic sculptures from there.
B Okay. But I just want to see the *Mona Lisa*.
A Open your mind a bit. The *Mona Lisa* is just one of the many great works of art at the Louvre.
B Okay. What are some other ones?
A Have you ever heard of the *Venus de Milo*?
B The *Venus de Milo* statue is here?
A That's right. There's a lot of great Renaissance art as well.
B You seem to know a lot about this museum. I'll follow you.
A Good idea. Let's get started.

Vocabulary

Match the words in the word box with the correct pictures.

drawing / sketch　portrait　photograph　painting
graffiti　architecture　sculpture　abstract

1.

2.

3.

4.

5.

6.

7.

8.

Listening

A Listen to the conversation and answer the questions. 10-02

1. In what country did Impressionism come to prominence?
   a. Spain
   b. England
   c. France

2. How did people feel about Impressionism when it first appeared?
   a. They didn't take the style seriously.
   b. They thought it was very respectable.
   c. They paid millions for paintings then.

3. What cannot be inferred about Impressionist paintings in the early 19th century?
   a. The painters preferred natural light-filled scenes.
   b. They were considered priceless and worthwhile.
   c. The paintings were not respected at the time.

4. What can be inferred about the painter of the painting?
   a. He enjoyed painting people in peaceful places.
   b. He had one daughter and one son.
   c. He often painted his mother and father.

B Listen again and choose True or False.

1. The painting depicts the painter's wife and child. [True / False]
2. Monet often painted unusual scenes and portraits. [True / False]
3. Impressionism is a style that tries to imitate the way light reflects off objects. [True / False]

Speaking

A Go online, find your favorite work of art, and complete the form.

Title ______________________

Painter ______________________

Year ______________________

Genre ______________________

Mood & Details ______________________

B Describe the work of art by using the form with the picture.

This painting is called *Ia Orana Maria*. It was painted by Paul Gauguin in 1891. It is a Victorian Era oil painting. His use of vivid and bright colors is impressive. Although the painting is set on the island of Tahiti, it actually portrays Christian religious themes. The yellow angel is pointing to a woman who is supposed to represent Mary, the mother of Jesus. The young son, of course, represents Jesus.

Venus of Willendorf

Conversation

Listen and practice the conversation. 10-03

A Vienna is such an amazing city.
B I know. Have you tried the apple strudel yet?
A I had some for breakfast. It was delicious.
B So where should we go first?
A I want to see the Venus of Willendorf. My professor talked about the sculpture in my anthropology class.
B Where is it?
A It's at the Vienna Natural History Museum.
B Okay. Why is the statue so famous?
A It's very old. It could be as many as 30,000 years old.
B What does it look like?
A It's a statue of a woman with exaggerated features. The large stomach and chest show the importance of fertility and childbearing during the Stone Age.
B That sounds really cool. It says here that the history museum is near the art museum, so we can visit both this morning.

Crossword Puzzle

Read the definitions, find the correct words and phrases in the conversation, and complete the puzzle.

Down
1 the social science that studies the origins and social relationships of human beings
2 a prominent attribute or aspect of something
3 the earliest known period of human culture, characterized by the use of stone implements
4 a thin sheet of filled dough rolled and baked

Across
5 a large sculpture of a person or an animal made of stone or metal
6 capable of producing offspring
7 represented as greater than is true or reasonable

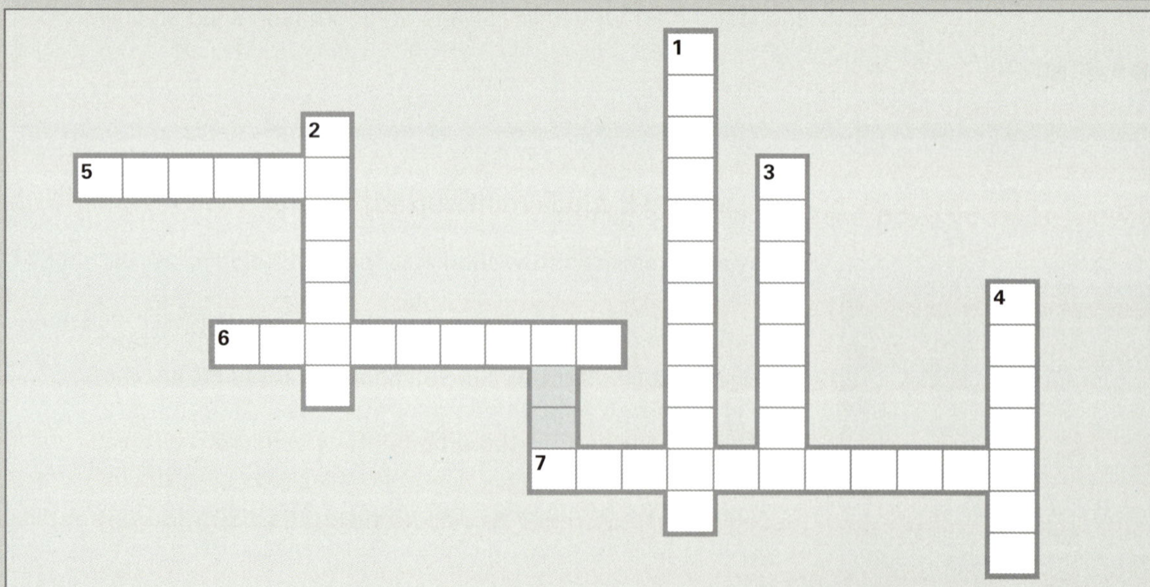

Listening

A Listen to the talk and answer the questions. 10-04

1. Where was *The Starry Night* painted?
   a. It was painted in Van Gogh's house.
   b. It was painted in a mental hospital.
   c. It was painted in Van Gogh's studio.

2. Who thinks Van Gogh lost his ear in an argument with a friend?
   a. two French artists
   b. some German historians
   c. Van Gogh and Gauguin

3. Why do the historians think Van Gogh didn't notify the police about the attack?
   a. He didn't want to get arrested.
   b. He wanted to punish his friend himself.
   c. He didn't want his friend to get into trouble.

4. What cannot be inferred?
   a. Van Gogh checked himself into the mental hospital after being attacked by his best friend.
   b. Van Gogh painted a masterpiece while he was going through a period of mental instability.
   c. Van Gogh avoided meeting Paul Gauguin even though they lived in the same neighborhood.

B Listen again and complete the table.

Title of Artwork: ______________________

Artist's Name	
Style	
Year	
Museum	*NY MoMA (New York Metropolitan Museum of Art)*

Pair Work

A Draw a school or park landscape in Box A. Then describe it to your partner while your partner draws a sketch of it in Box B. Take turns being the describer and the drawer.

A	B

B Whose drawing more closely resembles the original? Who's the better artist, you or your partner?

Street Art

Conversation

Listen and practice the conversation. 10-05

A Look at this graffiti. Some people have no respect for people's property.
B This isn't graffiti. It's street art. A famous artist did this.
A Really?
B Yeah. His name is Banksy.
A Is that his first name or last name?
B It's not his real name. His identity is actually a secret. He's an underground artist. He became famous by secretly putting graffiti art like this around London.
A Does he only do graffiti art?
B No, he makes sculptures, too. He's really creative.
A If he's so popular, how is his identity a secret?
B I don't know. I guess he has people that help him hide his identity.

Presentation

A Think about your favorite artist. Go online, learn about the artist, and complete the form.

Artist's Name	
Background - Birthdate - Hometown - Education	
Famous Artwork	
Style	
Awards	
Special Features	

B Make a presentation about your favorite artist to the class.

My favorite artist is El Greco. He was a Greek painter from the island of Crete and lived during the Renaissance. He moved to Venice, Italy, when he was 26 to train to become a master painter. He is famous for painting his subjects with unnaturally long fingers and strange skin tones. His style...

Listening

A Listen to the talk and correct the false sentences. 10-06

1. Frank Lloyd Wright's work has inspired younger generations for the past 60 years.
2. Wright's structures are in contrast to the environment.
3. Architecture was about conquering the environment in the 1920s.
4. The Empire State Building is an example of organic architecture.
5. Wright went in the same direction as his generation of architects.

B Complete the information about the home pictured below.

Architect	*Frank Lloyd Wright*
Name of Structure	
Year	
Location	*Southwestern Pennsylvania, USA*
Style	

Art Quiz

Go online and answer the questions.

ex. What's the most expensive painting ever sold? *Willem de Koonig's Interchange*

1. Where is the world's largest sculpture located?
2. Who is the richest living artist?
3. In which country did Picasso spend most of his adult life?
4. Name three characteristics of impressionist paintings.

A Strange Contest

Reading

A Read the article. 10-07

Rock, Scissors, Paper: An Art Auction Story

In 2005, the world's most expensive game of rock, scissors, papers was played between the two biggest auction houses in the world: Christy's and Sotheby's. A large Japanese electronics company named the Maspro Denkoh Corporation decided to sell its art collection, which included some very expensive pieces by artists such as Cezanne, Picasso, and Van Gogh. The sale was expected to raise as much as 20 million dollars at auction. The problem was that the CEO of the Maspro Denkoh Corporation, Takashi Hashayama, could not decide which auction house to use.

Both Christy's and Sotheby's had impeccable reputations, so there was no obvious choice for the beleaguered CEO. He decided to turn to an age-old children's game that has settled disputes on playgrounds across the world for generations: rock, scissors, paper.

The contest worked like this: Christy's and Sotheby's would have a few days to choose their weapon of choice. The auction houses' representatives would then meet with the company's reps. Each auction house rep would write their answer on a piece of paper, and the winner would be escorted downstairs to draw up paperwork for the auction. The winning auction house would receive approximately 12% of the money raised during the auction. That came out to a profit of more than one million dollars for the winner.

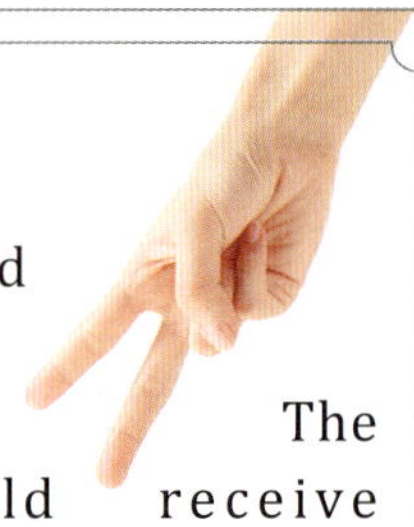

In the days before the contest, each auction house utilized different strategies to win. Sotheby's, figuring rock, scissors, paper is a game of chance, gave little thought to its choice. Christy's, however, consulted the children of one of its U.S. employees. The children said that everybody expects the other side to choose rock, so they should not choose rock. And the next obvious choice was paper because paper beats rock. The smartest choice, according to the kids, was scissors because scissors beats paper. The Christy's rep was sold on the children's strategy.

On the day of the contest, the two auction houses met, wrote their choices on slips of paper, and waited. Then, the company read the name of the winner: Christy's. Scissors beats paper. The children were right, and the rest was history.

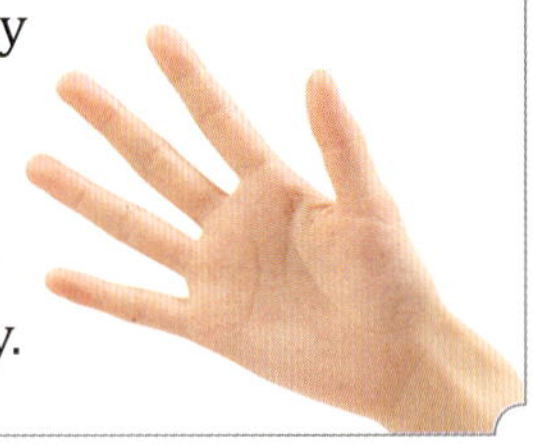

Comprehension Check Answer the questions about the article.

1. How much money was the auction expected to bring in?
2. Why couldn't the CEO decide between the two auction houses?
3. How did the CEO decide which auction house to use?
4. Why did the children want Christy's to choose scissors?

B Do you think playing rock, scissors, paper is a good way to make a big decision like this? Have you ever left an important decision to a game of chance?

Class Activity

A Make a group of four students. Then think about a famous artist and fill in the blanks with the information about him or her.

Artist's Name	
Country	
Famous Artwork	
Style	

B Choose a group representative and let him or her give a short presentation about the artist to the class.

C Choose one of the groups' presentations and write a summary about the group's artist using the prompts below.

Summarize: ________________ is a famous ________________ artist. ______________ is from ________________. ______________ is known for many popular ________________. A really famous ______________ of his is ________________________________. ______________ style of art is ________________________________.

Wrap-up

A Match the words with the correct definitions.

1. painting	•	•	a. a painting or a photograph of a person, usually the head and shoulders
2. photograph	•	•	b. the art of building design
3. drawing	•	•	c. a piece of art done with a pencil or charcoal
4. architecture	•	•	d. an unusual style of art where objects and faces may look distorted or strange
5. sculpture	•	•	e. a picture taken with a camera
6. portrait	•	•	f. a three-dimensional piece of art made with clay, metal, or other material
7. abstract	•	•	g. a piece of art created by using a brush and paint
8. graffiti	•	•	h. words or pictures that are written or drawn in public places; on walls or posters

B Refer to the questions to make a short presentation.

- What styles of art do you like? (paintings, sculptures, photographs, architecture, graffiti, etc.)
- What's your favorite work of art?
- Who's your favorite artist?
- What's your favorite artist's best piece of artwork?
- How do you feel when you see his / her artwork?

I like photographs. My favorite photograph is *The Vulture and the Little Girl*. It is Kevin Carter's Pulitzer Prize-winning photograph of a young starving Sudanese girl and a vulture in the background. Even though this picture is controversial, I think it is a significant piece of artwork because it raises awareness about the horrors of war.

C How do you feel about the pictures below? Share your thoughts and feelings about the pictures with a partner.

1.

2.

3.

Unit 11 Healthy Life Habits

Warm-up

Look at the pictures and compare the two men's lifestyles.

Tell me about your diet and lifestyle.

Conversation

Listen and practice the conversation. 11-01

A Jude, you look really healthy. What's your secret?
B There's no secret. I just eat a healthy diet, and I exercise. Oh, I also take supplements.
A I want to get healthy, too. What do you think I should do?
B Tell me about your lifestyle and diet, Lara.
A As you know, I have an office job, so I'm inside most of the day. I eat pretty well, but I only work out once or twice a week.
B What kind of workouts do you do?
A I jog for 20 to 30 minutes on a treadmill.
B Do you lift weights?
A Never.
B I think you should take some vitamin D because you're not getting enough sun. I would also strongly recommend you start lifting weights three times a week. Weightlifting not only builds muscle, but it also makes your bones stronger.
A Wow. Thanks for the great advice.

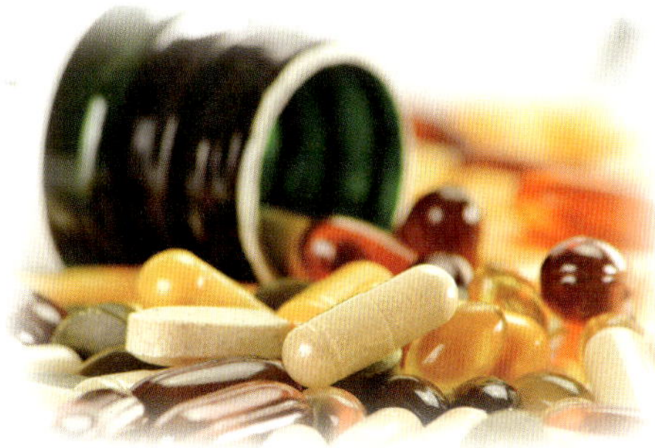

Pair Work

Healthy Habits

Ask your partner the questions in the questionnaire and add the scores from each question. Whose score is higher? Who lives a healthier life?

Healthy Habits Questionnaire			
1. How often do you exercise?			
Never	Once or twice a week	Three or four times a week	Almost every day
1	*2*	*3*	*4*
2. What do you think about your diet?			
Terrible	Okay	Not bad	Great
1	*2*	*3*	*4*
3. How much water do you drink a day?			
Hardly any	Almost half a liter	Almost a liter	One and a half to two liters
1	*2*	*3*	*4*
4. How long do you sleep?			
Fewer than four hours per night	Four to five hours per nigh	Six to seven hours per night	Seven to nine hours per night
1	*2*	*3*	*4*
		Total	____/16

Healthy (13 - 16)
Okay (9 - 12)
Needs Improvement (4 - 8)

A How often do you exercise?
B I exercise once or twice a week.

Listening

A Listen to the conversation and answer the questions. 11-02

1. How did Melissa get so thin?
   a. She started watching a TV show about diet.
   b. She saw a movie about proper nutrition.
   c. She read a popular book about nutrition.

2. What kinds of food are the foundation of Dr. Erickson's diet?
   a. fruits
   b. colorful vegetables
   c. leafy green vegetables

3. How much weight has Melissa lost?
   a. a bit of weight
   b. a fair amount of weight
   c. an incredible amount of weight

4. How will the man acquire the book?
   a. The woman will lend it to him.
   b. He will buy a copy.
   c. He's already purchased a copy.

B Listen again and choose True or False.

1. The man is surprised by the woman's weight loss. [True / False]
2. The man isn't really interested in the woman's weight-loss story. [True / False]
3. The woman mainly eats animal products with a few nuts and seeds. [True / False]
4. The woman doesn't think eating salads every day is boring. [True / False]
5. The man is interested in trying the diet, too. [True / False]

Pair Work

Food Journal

A Write down what you ate yesterday and find the number of calories each meal contained online. Then add the meals up and write the total number of calories in the table.

_________'s Food Journal

Breakfast		_______ kcal
Lunch		_______ kcal
Dinner		_______ kcal
Snacks		_______ kcal
	Total:	_______ kcal

B Compare your food journal with your partner's. Who consumed more calories?

I'm in!

Conversation

Listen and practice the conversation. 11-03

A Have you heard of X50 Plus?

B No, what's that?

A It's a workout program. I saw a commercial for it on TV last night.

B How does it work?

A You have to buy the DVDs. There are ten in total. It also comes with some exercise equipment, a diet guide, and worksheets.

B Did you buy it?

A No, not yet. But I wrote the phone number down.

B Are you going to buy it?

A I wanted to talk to you first. It's kind of expensive.

B How much is it?

A It's $129.99. But I thought if we did it together, we could cut the price in half.

B So we both chip in for it and follow the workouts together?

A Exactly. You've been talking about getting into shape. And I've wanted to get into shape for a while now. It seems perfect.

B Yeah, you're right. I'm in!

Words Search Puzzle

Find the words in the puzzle and circle them. Then match the words to the definitions.

1. workout **2.** commercial **3.** worksheet
4. equipment **5.** chip in **6.** exactly **7.** ~~shape~~

e	n	w	o	r	k	o	u	t	c
x	s	w	q	f	e	k	j	w	o
a	a	o	j	h	q	q	s	h	m
c	f	r	l	j	u	o	k	u	m
t	w	k	c	h	i	p	i	n	e
l	e	s	h	a	p	e	b	d	r
y	q	h	g	f	m	p	q	e	c
f	z	e	u	l	e	a	f	s	i
q	s	e	q	w	n	x	s	n	a
k	h	t	k	z	t	d	m	e	l

a. paper documents used to record work that has been planned or done on a project

b. exerting energy by using your muscles in various ways to keep fit

c. an advertisement that is broadcast on television, radio, or online

d. indicating exactness or preciseness

e. to collect money from each member of a group so the group can buy something together

f. items or machines needed to complete a specific job or activity

g. the visual appearance of something or someone

Listening

A Listen to the conversation and change the false statements into true statements. 11-04

1. Michael is 30 years old and 180cm tall.
2. The doctor would like to see Michael start eating processed foods.
3. Michael doesn't drink a lot of juice.
4. Michael plays basketball on Sundays.
5. Michael will see the doctor six months from now.

B Complete the table with the correct information.

	Michael's Lifestyle Now	New Health Plan for Michael
Number of Calories		*1800*
Diet	*processed foods and carbohydrates*	
Cardio Exercise		*30 minutes of cardio three times a week*
Weightlifting	*ten pushups every morning*	

TIPS & TIPS Use hyphens with ages in these situations.

The 12-year-old girl received a Christmas card from her grandmother. (age as an adjective before a noun)
That 40-year-old with the blue convertible is driving too fast. (age as a noun)

Survey

A Listen to the teacher read the statements out loud. Raise your hand if the statements are true for you. Then write in the table the number of students who raised their hands.

Diet & Exercise

Diet	How many	Exercise	How many
1. I am a vegetarian.		6. I enjoy playing sports.	
2. I am a meat lover.		7. I exercise regularly.	
3. I grow my own food.		8. I exercise occasionally.	
4. I love fast food.		9. I hate exercise.	
5. I often skip meals.		10. I have a gym membership.	

B How many students participated in the survey? Which statements did students agree with the most and the least?

How do you meditate?

Conversation

Listen and practice the conversation. 11-05

A You're always so composed, Summer, even when things are crazy around the office.

B I think the reasons are that I eat right and get regular exercise.

A I do, too, but I'm not as calm as you are. Little problems make me angry.

B Do you meditate?

A No. Do you?

B Absolutely. I meditate for 20 minutes every morning. It's one of the reasons I'm able to deal with the pressures of a busy office.

A Do I have to sit on the floor and chant?

B Don't be silly. All you have to do is sit in a chair with your back straight and concentrate on your breathing.

A It's that simple?

B It's that simple. And it will do wonders for your daily mood.

Vocabulary

Write the words in the correct places.

anxious cool dog-tired fatigued
nervous peaceful tired tranquil tense

1.

2.

3.

Listening

A Listen to the guided meditation and change the false statements into true statements. 11-06

1. Dr. Mark's office accepts credit cards, cash, and personal checks.
2. The woman must pay Dr. Mark directly.
3. The person who receives payments isn't the same person who schedules appointments.

B Choose the image that Cassandra sees in her mind.

1. 
2. 
3. 
4. 

Meditating

A Listen to the guided meditation and draw what comes to mind in as much detail as possible. 11-07

B Answer the questions about your meditation.

1. What beautiful place are you in? (beach, mountain, field, etc.)
2. What do you see?
3. What time of day is it?
4. Who, if anyone, is with you?
5. What are you doing there?
6. How do you feel?
7. Have you ever visited this place in your life?

C Write a short essay about your meditation by using the answers in B.

I'm a yoga teacher.

Reading

Read the interview. 11-08

Sunnyville Weekly Reader

June 3rd, 2018

People in Our City: A Yoga Instructor

M *Paula Martinez, thank you for talking with me today. As you know, the* Sunnyville Weekly Reader *interviews interesting people in our city. This week, we're talking to you because you have a very interesting job. Could you tell us about your job?*

P Sure. I'm a yoga instructor. I have my own yoga studio, and I teach classes in the mornings and evenings. I also have an early afternoon class for children.

M *Kids are doing yoga these days?*

P Oh, yeah. Yoga has become popular with people of all ages and genders. A lot of men are taking my yoga classes these days, too.

M *How did you first get into yoga?*

P My friend invited me to a yoga class many years ago, so I decided to go with him. I was an athlete in high school, so I thought it would be easy. Boy, was I wrong!

M *What do you mean?*

P It was really difficult. I couldn't hold the poses, and I kept taking breaks. That first yoga class almost killed me!

M *Hahaha! But you went back.*

P That's right. I saw it as a challenge. I needed to prove to myself that I could do it. Eventually, I got good at it.

M *How did you become a yoga instructor?*

P When the instructor of my class retired, I knew the studio needed to hire another one. So I applied for the job.

M *And you got it just like that?*

P I'd been an advanced student there for several years by then, so the owner knew I was capable. I taught the morning and evening classes and then worked my regular office job during the days.

M *Those must have been some long days.*

P They sure were! But I loved teaching yoga. The hard part was the office work. It was so boring.

M *How did you end up with your own studio?*

P I found an investor, a family friend. He offered to put up the money to help me get started. I had been teaching yoga part time for six years by then, so I knew how to run my own studio. It was very exciting to finally be teaching full time.

M *Wow, that's an incredible story. So how's business at your school?*

P Business is booming. We're opening a second school next month, and I'm hiring two new yoga instructors. The new teachers are just as passionate about yoga as I am.

Comprehension Check Answer the questions about the interview.

1. When does Paula teach yoga?
2. According to Paula, who is doing yoga these days?
3. What did Paula say about her first yoga class?
4. Who helped Paula get her own yoga studio?

At the Gym

Imagine you and your partner are at the gym. Choose a role as either a customer or a trainer. Then role-play by using the questions in the questionnaire. Take turns being the trainer.

Name ____________

Age ____________

☐ Male ☐ Female

---

1 What is the main reason you want to start exercising, to lose weight or to gain muscle? Or to improve your overall physical strength?

2 Have you done any strenuous exercise before?

☐ Yes ☐ No

3 How many times a week do you plan to come to the gym?

☐ once or twice a week

☐ three or four times a week

☐ almost every day

4 What time do you want to exercise, in the morning, afternoon, or evening?

☐ morning ☐ afternoon ☐ evening

5 Are there any supplementary classes you want to take, such as GX, Zumba, spinning, aerobics, or yoga?

☐ Yes ☐ No

6 Do you have any special requests or needs?

____

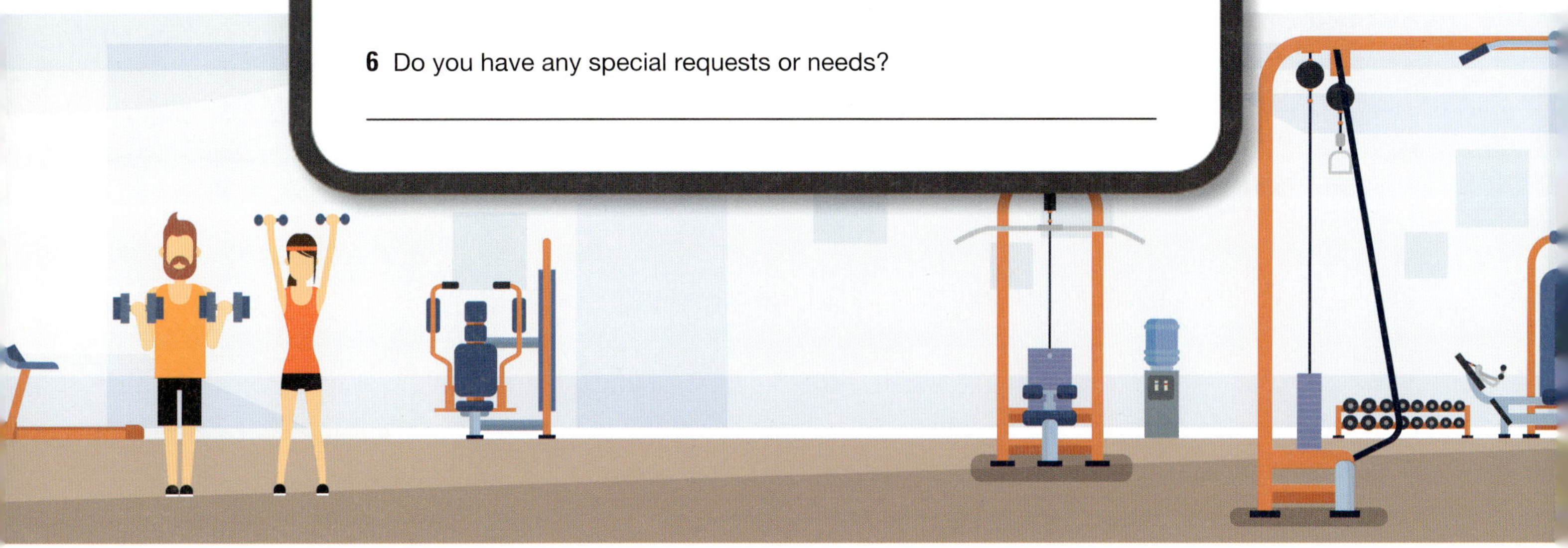

Wrap-up

A Look at the pictures and read the sentences. Then choose the correct words.

1.

Every morning, I do yoga. It makes me feel (peaceful / anxious).

2.

The entrance fee for the race is $100, but the winner gets $1,000 in prize money. If you (don't pay / chip in) $50, I'll give you half of the prize money if I win.

3.

The trainer at my gym is very diligent. She never forgets to make us complete our (registration forms / post-workout journals).

B How many calories do you think you consumed yesterday? Go online to help you determine the number of calories in each dish or drink.

Yesterday's Calorie Count

	Food Contents	Number of Calories
Breakfast		
Lunch		
Dinner		
Snacks / Drinks		
		Total: ________ kcal

C Read the statement below. Think of reasons why both sides of the argument could be true and write them in the table.

"Eating fast food once or twice a week is not harmful to your health."

I agree with the statement because...	I disagree with the statement because...

D Choose one side of the issue and debate a classmate by using the notes you wrote.

Unit **12**

Lucky Me!

Warm-up

A Look at the pictures. Check the ones that represent good luck.

B What are some examples of lucky or unlucky items in your culture?

I've won!

Conversation

Listen and practice the conversation. 12-01

A How can I help you, sir?
B I'd like one of those Lucky 7 scratch-off tickets.
A Okay. That'll be one dollar.
B Here you are.
A And here's your scratch-off ticket.
B Thanks. Do you mind if I scratch this off here?
A Not at all.
B Let's see. There's one seven... two sevens... three sevens! I've won!
A Oh, my goodness! How much did you win?
B I don't know. I have to scratch it off to see.
A So?
B Two dollars. I only won two dollars.
A Oh, that's too bad.
B Can I use this to buy two more tickets?
A Of course.

Questionnaire | Gambling

Ask your partner questions about gambling.

	yes	no
1. Is gambling legal in your country?	☐	☐
2. Does your country have casinos?	☐	☐
3. Have you ever been to a casino?	☐	☐
4. Do you consider yourself a lucky person?	☐	☐
5. Do you ever play cards for money with friends?	☐	☐
6. Do you know how to play poker?	☐	☐
7. Do you buy lottery tickets regularly?	☐	☐
8. Do you know anyone who has won money in the lottery?	☐	☐
9. What would you do if you won the lottery?		

Listening

A Listen to the conversation and answer the questions. 12-02

1. How much is the couple's monthly house payment including utilities?
   a. It's more than a thousand dollars.
   b. It's slightly less than a thousand dollars.
   c. It's slightly more than five hundred dollars.

2. How often does the couple make car insurance payments?
   a. They make yearly payments.
   b. They make biannual payments.
   c. They make payments twice every six months.

3. What is true about the man?
   a. He plans to have another job.
   b. He earns $1,900 per month including taxes.
   c. He needs $150 more every month.

4. What can be inferred about the woman?
   a. She needs to get promoted.
   b. She borrowed some money from her parents before.
   c. She will consider getting a part-time job.

B Listen to the rest of the conversation and choose True or False.

1. The man's new job is farther from his house than his old job. [True / False]
2. The man's boss told him he could be a general manager within ten years. [True / False]
3. The man will lead a team at his new job. [True / False]
4. The man's new job pays $200 per week more than his old job. [True / False]

Group Work Make a group of three or four students and ask about their lucky days.

Last Wednesday was a really lucky day for me. First, I found ten dollars on the street on my way to work. Then, my boss took me out for lunch. We had Japanese food. It was really good. On my way home from work, I didn't have to wait more than 30 seconds before the subway train arrived at the platform. It only took me fifteen minutes to get home!

What a horrible day!

Conversation

Listen and practice the conversation. 12-03

A Hello?

B Kristen, it's me, Jarrod. Can you pick me up at work? My car won't start.

A Of course. What happened?

B Jess broke up with me this morning.

A Oh, no. Why did she do that?

B Ever since I started this new job, I haven't been able to spend a lot of quality time with her. I think she felt neglected.

A That's too bad. I liked her.

B I couldn't concentrate today because of the breakup, and I forgot to send some important documents to my boss's client this morning.

A Oh, my goodness. What did you do?

B I drove to the client's office, which is about an hour away from my office. Because I was in such a hurry, I didn't have time to fill up the tank with gas. What a horrible day.

A Oh, I'm so sorry, Jarrod.

Speaking

Choose one of the pictures and say what you think happened. Then say how you would feel and what you would do if you were the person. Answers may vary.

The man spilled coffee on his white shirt. I'd be really frustrated. I would go home and change my shirt. I hate wearing shirts with stains on them.

Listening

A Listen to the three speakers and choose True or False. If the statement is false, change it to make it true.

12-04

1-2

1. Tim arrived late on his first day of work. [True / False]
2. Tim's boss yelled at him for half an hour. [True / False]

3-4

3. Angela's presentation took about forty-five minutes. [True / False]
4. Angela left her USB in her office. [True / False]

5-6

5. Ryan dated his girlfriend for about three years. [True / False]
6. Ryan spotted his ex-girlfriend near the back of the line. [True / False]

B Complete the table with the correct information.

1.
Where:
When: *twenty years ago*
What Happened:

2.
Where: *in the boardroom*
When:
What Happened:

3.
Where:
When: *last week*
What Happened:

Speaking

A Think about a bad day you had and answer the questions.

- When was it?
- Where were you?
- Who were you with?
- What happened?
- How did you respond?

B Tell your partner about your bad day by using the answers in A.

I had a bad day last Monday. I was at the office, and I was talking to my colleague when I suddenly spilled coffee on my brand-new white shirt. I immediately tried to clean it in the washroom, but the stain didn't come out. I had to wear a jacket all day long to cover up the stain, but it was really warm in the office. I was sweaty and uncomfortable the whole day.

You make your own luck.

Conversation

Listen and practice the conversation. 12-05

A Your house is enormous!
B Well, there are five bedrooms and three bathrooms. I guess that's pretty big.
A I live in a studio apartment downtown. And I have a roommate!
B Oh, I see.
A Is that a swimming pool?
B We thought the kids would enjoy it in the summertime.
A And a hot tub, too! You're so lucky.
B What do you mean?
A You're a lucky guy. You're only 30, and you have all of this.
B My wife and I worked hard to buy this house. Luck had nothing to do with it.
A I'm sorry. I didn't mean to offend you.
B It's all right. It's just that I don't believe in luck. I think you make your own luck.
A How do you do that?
B You set a goal, and then you don't stop working hard until you achieve it.

Discussion | Rules to Live By

Make a group of four students and discuss each member's top five rules to live by (work hard, tell the truth, make your own luck, etc.). Then decide on one master list of five rules to live by and complete the chart.

Top 5 Rules to Live By

1.	
2.	
3.	
4.	
5.	

Class Activity

A Think about the luckiest person you know and answer the questions.

- What is the name of the person?
- Why do you think the person is lucky?

B Make a group of four students. Tell your group about the luckiest person you know. Then listen and take notes about the luckiest people your group members know.

Name	What the Person's Name Is	Why This Person Is Lucky
Me		

C Vote on who you think the luckiest person is. Then choose a group representative and let him or her make a presentation about the person to the class.

Luck vs. Attitude

Reading

A Read the online editorial. 12-06

www.financeweekly.com

Career Success: Luck or Attitude

Staff Writer **Cameron Blackman**

Something many of us have wondered about successful people is how much of their success can be attributed to luck. It is easy for us to look at millionaires and billionaires and to decide that they are lucky while we are not so lucky. They don't work harder than we do. Rather, they just caught a few lucky breaks along the way, and that's life. But some experts believe this attitude may be the exact reason why some people are successful and others are not. These experts have found that what looks like dumb luck from an outsider's perspective is actually a healthy and systematic pattern of behavior and attitudes that successful people utilize in order to get ahead in life, especially in the business world.

The first example they found was that successful people don't simply fall into fortunate situations, but, instead, they create fortunate situations. Lucky people don't wait around for lady luck to come knocking at their door. They go out and find her. Ask any successful people about their week, and they will tell you about numerous projects they recently finished, are in the process of finishing, or plan to start. And it's not that successful people are all workaholics or money-hungry barbarians. The secret successful people have discovered is that the more attempts they have at a target, the better their chances are of hitting the bullseye. Successful people take lots of chances, and if one out of ten is a success, then great!

And that brings us to the second thing that differentiates successful people from the less successful: failure. Successful people are not afraid of failure. Steve Jobs and his partner Steve Wozniak, practically blew up his parent's garage in an attempt to build the first personal computer. But they never stopped even when things looked really bleak.

The final behavior that sets successful people apart from the rest of us is their optimism. Successful people believe in themselves and their ideas. And this idea makes a lot of sense. If you don't believe in your own idea, why should anyone else? So if you want become a successful person, adopt these three principles into your professional lives and watch as you transform from an average Joe into a business elite.

Comprehension Check Answer the questions about the online editorial.

1. What have experts discovered about luck?
2. What are three things successful people do?
3. Why did the author use Steve Jobs and Steve Wozniak as examples?
4. What does the author think will happen to people if they adopt these principles?

B Do you think you are a successful person? Do you have the three traits for success discussed in the text?

Group Work

Who is the luckiest person?

Make a group of four or five students. Discuss the four options and make your own choices. Then talk about your choices.

1. a great job vs. a great spouse
2. an expensive sports car vs. a healthy body
3. a high-paying job with lots of hours vs. an okay-paying job with few hours
4. living in a mansion alone vs. living in an apartment with a loving family
5. ? vs. ?

I'd rather have a great job. I can find a spouse when I'm older. Much older!

Which would you rather have, Kelly: a great job or a great spouse?

Wrap-up

A Complete the conversation with the correct words.

gambling	a lucky break	fortune	lottery

A I just bought a ______________ ticket.
B Really? I don't like ______________.
A I feel lucky today.
B Not me. I can't seem to ever catch ______________.
A What do you mean? You have a great job and a wonderful family.
B When you put it that way. I guess you're right. I have had some good ______________ in my life.
A You've got that right!

B Conduct a short survey about luck and use the data from your survey to give a short presentation about luck.

Question 1. Do you think you are lucky?
Question 2. If yes, what's the reason?

More than half of the students thought they were lucky. Their reasons varied. Two people said they were lucky because they found some money. One person said she was lucky because she found a nice boyfriend.

C Choose a side and take notes on the reasons that support your side.

People are successful because they are lucky.	People are successful because they work hard.

D Use your notes from C in order to write a short essay.

Answer Key

Answer Key

Unit 1 Life and Learning

Warm-up p. 11

1. c
2. e
3. a
4. b
5. d

Orientation Day

Vocabulary p. 12

1. psychology
2. accounting
3. journalism
4. biology
5. chemistry
6. electronic engineering
7. philosophy
8. history

Listening p. 13

Script

A: Hey, are you Elena?

B: Yeah? Are you Kelly?

A: Yes, I am. It's nice to meet you.

B: Nice to meet you, too.

A: What's your major?

B: Psychology. How about you?

A: I'm undecided right now. I'm going to take some general courses before I choose a major.

B: Cool. Well, I chose the bed next to the window, so I guess the other one is yours.

A: Okay, that's cool. Do you have a television?

B: No, I don't.

A: No problem. I brought one.

B: I brought a computer printer. You can use it anytime you need to.

A: Great. Did you bring a microwave?

B: No, unfortunately I didn't.

A: That's okay. My aunt has an old one she said I could have. I'll get it from her when I go home for the weekend. Hmm, is there anything else we need? Do you play video games?

B: My brother wouldn't let me bring our Xbox from home. I'm so depressed.

A: Guess what? I've brought mine! Let's get it from my car.

B: Yay! I think we're going to get along really well.

A: Me, too!

B: After we get your Xbox, I'll introduce you to the other girls on the floor.

A: Cool. I can't wait to meet them.

A

1. c
2. a
3. a
4. b

B

1. False
2. True
3. False
4. False

A Club Meeting

Listening p. 15

Script

A: What clubs did you belong to when you were a university student?

B: I was in the school choir and the badminton club.

A: Wow! You're musical and athletic.

B: I wasn't very good at badminton though. I just really enjoyed playing.

A: Do you play now?

B: No, not really. My husband and I play only once a month.

A: Do you still sing?

B: Yes, absolutely! I sing in the church choir every Sunday. We meet three times a week to practice.

A: Three nights a week?

B: That's right. We practice on Mondays, Wednesdays, and Thursdays. Then, we perform on Sunday mornings. How about you? What clubs did you belong to in college?

A: I was kind of nerdy.

B: What do you mean?

A: I was a member of two clubs. One was called Mathletes, and the other was called the United Nations club.

B: What was the Mathletes club?

A: We met twice a week in the evenings and solved complicated mathematical problems. There were two teams, and the first team to solve the problem received a point. We also competed against other schools.

B: That's cool.

A: Cool isn't exactly the right word to describe it. But it was fun. And I met my wife in the club.

B: That's awesome. What did you do in the United Nations club?

A: Each member would represent a different country from the United Nations. Then, we would debate global issues and try to find diplomatic solutions to difficult world problems. We met three times a week, so I was busy every evening in college.

B: I can see why you liked those clubs. You're such a smart person.

A: Well, thanks. I still enjoy reading about politics, and as an engineer, I use math from Monday to Friday.

A

1. c
2. b
3. c
4. a
5. b

B

	Sun	Mon	Tue	Wed	Thu	Fri	Sat
Woman	√	√		√	√		
Man		√	√	√	√	√	

Lai plays chess on Saturdays.

Useful Expressions p. 16

B

1. Paul and Elizabeth volunteer to pick up litter every morning.
2. Simon and Jane play tennis three times a week.
3. The students study Italian on weekdays.
4. Harold takes a walk with his dog twice a day.
5. Mariel cooks most evenings.

Listening p. 17

Script

A: Did you go to the campus festival last night?

B: No, I didn't. Who organized the event?

A: The student events committee organized the festival.

B: How was it?

A: It was great. There were games with prizes, lots of food and drinks, and live music.

B: What kind of food did they have?

A: Tacos, burritos, pizza, popcorn, and cotton candy.

B: Did they serve any alcohol?

A: No, they only served nonalcoholic drinks like soda, juice, and energy drinks.

B: I see. You said there was music. Who performed last night?

A: The rapper G-Luv performed. He performed for about an hour and a half.

B: Cool. Did you like it?

A: It was great. A new female artist opened for him. Her name is Angel Ramirez. No one knew who she was, but she sang really well.

B: It's too bad I missed it. I'm definitely going to the committee's next festival.

A: There's another one in October.

B: Great!

A

1. b 2. c 3. b

B

1. False 2. True 3. False
4. False 5. True

First Impressions

Reading p. 18

Comprehension Check

1. It is often the correct one.
2. Humans needed to react to dangerous situations.
3. Don't ignore your feelings.
4. A person might miss out on a good business or relationship opportunity.
5. By learning how to get in touch with our feelings

Listening p. 19

Script

1. A: Sandy, Mr. Pearson will see you now.
   B: Great. Thanks.
   C: Hello, Sandy. Please have a seat.
   B: Okay. Hi. I'm happy to be here today. I'm sorry, but I'm a little nervous. This is my first job interview.
2. A: Ted, Mr. Pearson will see you now.
   B: Great. Thanks.
   C: Hello, Ted. Please have a seat.
   B: Hello. Thank you for seeing me this afternoon. It's a pleasure to meet you.
3. A: Elliot, Mr. Pearson will see you now.
   B: Great. Thanks.
   C: Hello, Elliot. Please have a seat.
   B: Hey, what's up, man! Whoa, you have a cool office.

Wrap-up p. 20

A

1. philosophy 2. accounting
3. journalism 4. psychology
5. electronic engineering

B

1. skilled 2. not good
3. talented 4. good
5. poor

Unit 2 Stress

He keeps giving me his work!

Listening p. 23

Script

1. Hi, my name's Juanita. I like my job, but there's just one problem. My boss gives me too much work. I can't finish it all in one day. Then, the next day, he gives me too much work

again, so I have to do that work and the work from the day before. The papers keep piling up on my desk, and I have to work every Saturday just to finish the week's work. Don't get me wrong. I like my job, and I make a good salary. But I have no free time. I would love to sleep late on Saturday just one time!

2. Hey, I'm Mitchell. I have a pretty big problem at work. My boss keeps asking me to go to dinner with her. Now don't get me wrong. She's smart, interesting, and attractive, too. But I just feel really uncomfortable going on a date with my boss. What would my coworkers think? Last week, she made me the project manager of a really important client's deal. Did she do that because she likes me or because she thinks I'm a good worker?

3. Hi, my name's Dana. I have a great career. I'm an executive at a very successful company. I make lots of money and own a very nice apartment in the center of the city. But I'm lonely. There's a guy in my office that I really like. He's smart and handsome. I've asked him to dinner a few times, but he always says he's busy. I think he's afraid to go on a date with his boss. But who cares! It's possible to separate work and social life, right?

A

1. b 2. c 3. b
4. c 5. a

B

1. Saturday 2. project
3. possible 4. career

The baby's crying.

Grammar p. 24

B

1. so 2. such 3. such
4. so 5. such

Listening p. 25

Script

A: How was your weekend, Eileen?

B: Don't ask, Jim!

A: That bad, huh?

B: It was so hectic. On Friday night, after I got home from work, we went to Isabelle's piano recital. Then, on Saturday morning, Patrick had a soccer game. And in the afternoon, Isabelle's classmate had a birthday party.

A: Wow, that was a busy weekend.

B: That's not the end of it. My husband's company had a picnic on Sunday afternoon, so I had to prepare a bunch of sandwiches in the morning.

A: I hope your husband appreciated your hard work.

B: He did. He's taking the kids to a baseball game next weekend, so I can have the house to myself.

A: That's great. And don't worry. It gets so much easier as the children get older. My teenagers are always busy doing school activities or going to the mall with their friends. They never want to spend time with my wife and me. We kind of miss how things used to be.

B: Yeah, I guess I really need to enjoy my time with the kids while they're young.

A

1. b 2. a 3. b
4. b 5. c

B

	Friday	Saturday	Sunday
A.M.	Work	Patrick's Soccer Game	Preparing a Bunch of Sandwiches
P.M.	Isabelle's Recital	Isabelle's Friend's Birthday Party	My Husband's Company Picnic

You could have done it then.

Grammar p. 26

B

1. while 2. by 3. until
4. during 5. for

C

1. Suji listened to music while studying yesterday.
2. Paul asked his teacher a question during class this morning.
3. Demian has played the guitar for three years.
4. You have until next Friday to submit the report.

Listening p. 27

Script

A: What am I going to do?

B: What's wrong, Barbara?

A: I have a huge project due tomorrow in my food and nutrition class.

B: When did you get the assignment?

A: Three weeks ago.

B: Really? So how much have you finished already?

A: Nothing. I put it off for weeks, and now I'm afraid it's too late.

B: What exactly do you have to do?

A: I'm supposed to interview a person about his or her diet and exercise routine. Then, I'm supposed to write a report.

B: What kind of report do you have to write?

A: I need to create a diet plan and exercise routine for the person.

B: Why don't you interview me? I can help you finish it this evening.

A: Really? You'd do that for me?

B: Sure. I'd love to learn more about nutrition and dieting. I might even use your recommendations to lose some weight and to build some muscle.

A: Thank you, Carla. I owe you big time!

A

1. b	2. b	3. a
4. c	5. b	

B

1. Barbara has not yet started the project.
2. Barbara put off doing the assignment for weeks.
3. Barbara has to interview a person about his or her diet and exercise routine.
4. Barbara is going to interview Carla.

Healthy Life

Reading p. 28

Comprehension Check

1. It's a summary of a book.
2. Evan Handley wrote *The Stress Test*.
3. Stress produces cortisol, which interferes with the body's ability to fight infections.
4. Stress causes arterial walls to thicken.
5. Stress causes too much bad bacteria to grow.

Wrap-up p. 30

A

1. gossip	2. loud talker
3. bully	4. lunch thief
5. know-it-all	6. cubicle invader

B

1. It's so hot. I think it's over 40 degrees.
2. They are such good dancers. They won a dance contest.
3. He's so good at surfing. He goes surfing every summer.
4. She's such a workaholic. She works over 80 hours a week.

C

1. by	2. until	3. during

Unit 3 Entertainment

Can you help me download it?

Grammar p. 32

B

1. b	2. b	3. a
4. b		

Listening p. 33

Script

A: Quickly! Give me your phone. I left mine in the car.

B: Why do you need my phone?

A: I want to record the show. This comedian is really funny. I'm going to put the video on my UTube channel.

B: No way! You're not allowed to record the performers.

A: Why not?

B: It's illegal. You need permission from the performer. Did he say you could post a video of his performance?

A: No. But who cares? People do it all the time.

B: I care.

A: Oh, look. The performance is almost finished. It's too late. We missed it.

B: Can I have the car keys?

A: The car keys? Why?

B: I'm going to wait in the car.

A: Oh, no. Wait. I'm sorry!

A

1. c	2. a	3. b
4. c	5. a	

B

1. True	2. False	3. True
4. False		

Do you like comedies?

Vocabulary p. 34

1. romance	2. horror	3. action
4. historical drama	5. science fiction	6. comedy
7. crime drama	8. Western	

Listening p. 35

Script

1. A: What did you think of the movie?

   B: It was all right. I didn't really like the ending very much.

   A: The ending was the best part! What didn't you like about it?

   B: The superhero defeated the villain.

A: So?

B: I'd like to see a movie where the superhero loses.

A: Oh, my gosh! That's ridiculous. You can't make a superhero movie where the superhero loses.

B: Why not?

A: Because the whole point of superhero movies is that the hero wins. That's why they call him a superhero!

2. A: I love Woody Allen films. They're so funny and smart.

B: What's your favorite Woody Allen film?

A: I really love *Crimes and Misdemeanors*, but *Annie Hall* is definitely my favorite.

B: Those movies are kind of old. I like his newer films.

A: Which newer film of his is your favorite?

B: I loved *Midnight in Paris*. It's such a charming fantasy film.

A: I agree. It was fantastic. I saw it in the theater two times.

3. A: Aaaah! I can't look!

B: Are you okay?

A: This movie is too scary. I can't take it.

B: Do you want to leave the theater?

A: No. I have a better idea.

B: What's that?

A: Since you've already seen this movie, can you tell me when a scary part is coming up? Then, I'll cover my eyes.

B: Sure. Good idea. By the way, there's a scary part coming up in about a minute.

1. b	2. True	3. b
4. True	5. False	6. c
7. False		

A Sport Podcast

Grammar p. 36

B

1. what time the movie starts
2. Maria is coming to the party
3. when summer vacation begins
4. how I should solve it
5. we needed an extra day

Listening p. 37

Script

A: Sophia, could you tell me why this isn't working?

B: What are you trying to do?

A: I'm trying to create my own OnTube channel. I saw yours, and I thought it looked really cool, so I wanted to make one, too.

B: My channel is about dieting and exercise. I didn't know you were interested in those topics.

A: Actually, I'm not. I would like to create a OnTube channel where I review new video games.

B: Oh, I see. Of course, I can help you. Let's see. Creating a channel is easy. Create an account and go to My Channel.

A: Okay, I did that.

B: Now, click on the "Channel Art" button and add some photos if you want to. You can also add some different colors and designs to the page.

A: Oh, I see. Cool. How do you make your videos?

B: I just use the camera on my phone. I use a tripod, so the camera doesn't move too much. And I edit my videos by using the OnTube Video Editor app. You can download it at the Tooble Playstore.

A: Great! Thanks a lot Sophia. When I'm finished, can you tell me what you think about my channel?

B: Of course! I can't wait.

A

1. c	2. a	3. c
4. b		

B

1. nutrition and diet	2. old
3. a phone camera	4. tool

The New Radio

Reading p. 38

Comprehension Check

1. It has been declining.
2. A person needs an Internet connection and a media device that plays MP3 files.
3. There are podcasts for almost every topic.
4. Podcasters have more freedom and fewer rules.
5. He conducted the interview in his garage.

Wrap-up p. 40

A

1. comedy	2. science fiction
3. horror	4. romance

B

1. horror	2. comedy
3. romance	4. Science fiction

C

1. Can you tell me how much water you drink a day?
2. Is Bill coming to the party?
3. Do you know whether or not Alan goes to the bank on Tuesdays?
4. What time is it?

Unit 4 Conflict

I totally disagree!

Useful Expressions p. 42

B

1. b 2. a 3. c

C

(Example Answer)
I totally agree. Watching scary horror movies is stressful. / I beg to differ. It's thrilling for me to watch scary horror movies.

Listening p. 43

Script

1. A: Are Debbie and Jerry coming over for dinner on Friday evening?
   B: Yes, they are.
   A: We should buy some meat. A barbecue on the patio would be a lot of fun.
   B: I don't think so. It's too cold outside these days.
   A: Not necessarily. If we all wear warm clothes, we'll be fine.
   B: Let's have lasagna inside. It'll be more comfortable for everybody.
   A: You're probably right. Let's do that.
2. A: We need to arrange a date and time for our next meeting.
   B: Next Tuesday at 11:00 a.m. is good for me.
   A: I'm afraid that won't work for me. How about Tuesday afternoon?
   B: Oh, I'm sorry. I have to meet clients on Tuesday afternoon.
   A: Oh, that's too bad.
   B: Is next Wednesday bad for you?
   A: Not necessarily. I could move some of my Wednesday appointments around. What time do you want to meet on Wednesday?
   B: How about at 2:00 p.m.?
   A: Okay, that's fine. Let's meet next Wednesday at 2:00 p.m.
3. A: This book is so good! You have to read it.
   B: What book is it?
   A: It's called *Stand Alone*. It's a new novel by Katherine McKinny. She's a brilliant author.
   B: I couldn't agree more! I love her books.
   A: Her first book, *Firestorm*, was my favorite until I read this new one. Do you want to read my copy when I'm finished with it?
   B: Absolutely. But don't tell me anything about it. I want to be surprised.
   A: Okay. Got it.

1. c 2. False 3. a
4. True 5. False 6. c
7. False

I've got a big problem.

Useful Expressions p. 44

B

1. A: I am going to meet Angela for some pizza and beer. Do you want to join us?
   B: Absolutely. How do you feel about going to Queen's Pizza? It just opened last week. I heard from my co-worker that the pizza there tastes great.
   A: I know that place. It looks a little expensive though. You told me that you're going to cut back on spending. Honestly, I think we should choose Kim's Pizza Factory.
2. A: What do you think about my dress?
   B: You look amazing. Where are you going in that fancy dress?
   A: I'm not going anywhere. My boyfriend is going to make a video call to me soon.
   B: In that case, I think a dress is too much then.
3. A: Minji just called me and asked me to go out tonight.
   B: That sounds great.
   A: But I have an English test tomorrow...
   B: If I were you, I would stay home and prepare for the test.

Listening p. 45

Script

A: What's that?
B: It's Anna and Eric's wedding invitation.
A: Oh, great! When is it?
B: It's on July 2nd at 2:00 p.m.
A: Oh, no! That's the same day as my mother's birthday.
B: I know. What do you think we should do?
A: Well, I can't skip my mother's birthday.
B: And I can't miss my best friend's wedding.
A: If you ask me, I think you should go to the wedding, and I should go to the birthday party.
B: But we won't be together.
A: Where's the wedding?
B: It's at St. Peter's Church.
A: That's only fifteen minutes from my mother's house. How about if I visit my mother in the morning and meet you at St. Peter's Church at two o'clock?
B: Good idea. Then what do you want to eat at the wedding, tomato pasta or cream pasta?
A: Definitely cream pasta.
B: Me, too. Two cream pastas then.

A

Wedding Invitation

Anna Dempsey & Eric Johnson

Date	July 2nd
Time	2:00 p.m.
Place	St. Peter's Church
Guest	yes ☑ no ☐
Meal	Tomato Pasta ☐ Cream Pasta ☑

B

1. True 2. False 3. False
4. False

It's so annoying!

Listening p. 47

Script

A: Philip, you're late again.

B: I'm sorry, Ms. Graves. Traffic this morning was terrible.

A: That's what you said yesterday and the day before yesterday.

B: I know, but it was bumper to bumper.

A: I'm sure it was. But that's three times this week, and it's only Thursday! And as you know, your annual performance review is coming up in a few weeks.

B: I won't be late tomorrow, Ms. Graves. I promise.

A: I hope not.

A

1. a 2. b 3. b
4. c

Script

A: Philip, can I see you in my office, please?

B: Of course, Ms. Graves.

A: You were late again this morning. I'm very disappointed.

B: Honestly, I just can't make it here on time. I live quite far from the office.

A: What do you think we should do?

B: Is it possible for me to start work at 8:30 a.m. instead of at 8:00 a.m.? Then I could leave the office at 5:30 p.m. instead of at 5:00 p.m.

A: Hmm. That's an interesting proposal. How far is your house from the office?

B: It's about 60 kilometers.

A: That is quite far. All right, I can make an exception in your case. You'll start half an hour later in the morning but stay half an hour later in the evening.

B: Thank you, Ms. Graves. I really appreciate it.

A: You're welcome. Don't forget about your performance review on the 22nd.

B: Okay, I won't forget.

B

1. False 2. True 3. True

Break Room Memos

Reading p. 48

Comprehension Check

1. She put her name on the paper bag.
2. She went out for lunch.
3. They should recycle the bottles and cans.
4. They clean the office in the evenings.
5. They should call Michael. His extension is 1124.

Unit 5 Fashion and Personal Style

I want to go to the outlet mall.

Vocabulary p. 52

1. a steal 2. a flea market 3. an outlet mall
4. a yard sale 5. a rip-off 6. a fitting room
7. brand name 8. e-commerce 9. off-brand

Listening p. 53

Script

1. A: Matt, help me carry these boxes outside. You can put them in the front yard?

B: What are they for, Clair?

A: They're for the garage sale.

B: When is the garage sale?

A: Today! I told you about it a week ago.

B: Oh... Hey, my comic books are in this box!

A: You never read them, and I'm sick and tired of them taking up space in our house.

B: All right. But you can't sell my video games. I love these games.

A: You're 37 years old. You're too old to play video games. Besides, you haven't played these games in years.

B: Wait a minute! Are those my fishing rods? You can't sell my fishing rods!

2. A: Oh, my gosh! That Luis Belvoir handbag is 70% off.

B: I know, but it's still $400. What are you going to do?

A: I think I have to buy it. I love the design.

B: Why is it 70% off?

A: It's last year's design. But I don't care. Luis Belvoir handbags are timeless.

B: That's true. But what's wrong with your current handbag?

A: This old thing. It's generic. I bought it at an outlet mall a couple of years ago.

B: It looks expensive though.

A: I know. But I want to have a brand-name handbag. The problem is it's still expensive. Brad's going to be really angry if I spend $400. I told him he couldn't buy a $100 golf club last week because we didn't have the money.

B: What are you going to do?

A: Whatever! I'm going to put it on my credit card. You only live once, you know!

3. A: Is this your first time at the Centerville Flea Market?

B: No, I came here last year. By the way, how much is this lamp?

A: It's $25.00.

B: Isn't that a little expensive? How about $10.00?

A: $10.00? No way! That's a nice lamp. I can't sell it for any less than $20.00.

B: Well, I guess I could go as high as $15.00.

A: Fifteen is a steal.

B: Twenty is a rip-off.

A: Let's meet in the middle. How about $17.50?

B: $17.50? All right, deal!

A

1. a	2. b	3. b

B

1. 37	2. 400	3. 100
4. 17.50		

I need a new look.

Vocabulary p. 54

A

1. chic	2. vintage
3. thrift store	4. casual / dressed down
5. dressed up	6. dress for the occasion
7. off-the-peg / off-the-rack	8. the latest trend

Listening p. 55

Script

1. A: How would you describe your style, Britney?

B: I would describe my style as casual and cool. I love to wear my skinny jeans. I think they look good on me. I'm a university student, so I don't need to dress up very often. I usually wear sleeveless shirts because I want my arms to be tan. I wear my hair long past my shoulders because I think long hair is beautiful. And my boyfriend likes it long, too!

2. A: Tell me about your style, Kyle.

B: My style is pretty normal or average. I mean, I don't wear anything special. I'm a T-shirt and jeans kind of guy, you know. I have a lot of T-shirts—probably over fifty of them. Sometimes I go to thrift shops to look for cool or interesting T-shirts. My favorite T-shirt is my Tool T-shirt. They're my favorite rock band. I got it at their concert last year. I wear it at least once a week.

3. A: Can you tell us about your style, Francine?

B: Of course. I'd love to. Just like Britney, my favorite pants are my skinny jeans. I'm a bit more conservative than she is because I don't like wearing sleeveless shirts. Since it's hot here in Austin, Texas, I usually wear T-shirts. But I don't have as many as Kyle! I have about ten T-shirts. I wear my hair short because it's hot here. When I was younger, I hated the fact that I had to wear glasses. Now I like wearing glasses. I bought these fashionable frames at a local glasses shop. I think they make my face look good. My friends say I look like a hipster, but I don't mind. I think it is a compliment.

1. a	2. c	3. c
4. c	5. b	6. c

Can I borrow your red vest?

Listening p. 57

Script

A: Ugh, I'm so frustrated!

B: What's wrong, Mindy?

A: Pablo wore track pants, sneakers, and a T-shirt to dinner last night. Can you believe it? It was Valentine's Day, and we had reservations at Le Grande, the new French restaurant downtown. I was so embarrassed by him. He said he wore those clothes because he had been at the gym before he came to the restaurant.

B: Men are strange. Maybe he didn't realize he was supposed to dress up.

A: I told him like ten times! I even sent him a text message reminding him to wear his blue suit. He looks handsome in his blue suit.

B: Maybe he did it on purpose.

A: On purpose? What do you mean?

B: Maybe he thinks you are too controlling. He might think you treat him like a child by telling him what to wear. So he wore the most inappropriate outfit to make you angry.

A: Hmm. I guess it's possible. I can be quite controlling sometimes. Why can't he just talk to me when he's upset?

B: You're right. He should have talked to you. I think the two of you need to have a serious discussion.

A: You're right. I'm going to talk to him about this tomorrow.

A

1. b　　2. b　　3. c
4. a

B

1. Mindy and Pablo went to dinner on Valentine's Day.
2. Mindy and Pablo met at La Grande, the new French restaurant.
3. Mindy was very embarrassed by the way Pablo looked at dinner.
4. X
5. Pablo might think Mindy treats him like a child.

Three Year Ago vs. Now

Reading p. 58

Comprehension Check

1. She didn't have the right clothes.
2. She lived in the Bronx. Now she lives in Manhattan.
3. She had a roommate in 2010, but now she lives in a good-sized apartment all by herself.
4. Now she wears designer suits.
5. He's a stockbroker.

Wrap-up p. 60

A

designer, yard sale, a steal, the outlet mall, ripped off

Unit 6 Immigration and Life Abroad

Warm-up p. 61

A

1. b　　2. c　　3. d
4. a

Have you gotten your visa yet?

Vocabulary p. 62

1. b　　2. a　　3. c
4. a　　5. b

Listening p. 63

Script

A: Excuse me, Professor Mackey. I'm really interested in the year-long study abroad program in Beijing. But I'm not sure what I need to do in order to apply for it.

B: That's great, Cassandra. Well, the first thing you need to do is to get an application form from the registrar's office.

A: Oh, okay. What else do I need?

B: Well, there's some information you're going to need to collect in order to complete the form. For example, you'll need a CLFE score.

A: A CLFE score? What's that?

B: CLFE stands for the Chinese Language Fluency Exam. A level 2 or above means you have a basic understanding of conversational Chinese. Do you think you can get to level 2?

A: I've been studying Mandarin for three years, so I don't think it will be a problem.

B: Great. You'll also need a letter of recommendation from a professor at our school.

A: Professor Mackey, would you please write me a letter of recommendation?

B: Of course, I'd be happy to. And you'll need to write a 500-word essay about why you should be accepted into the program.

A: I'm really interested in Asian culture, especially the history. And I'm really interested in...

B: Whoa, Cassandra, save it for the essay.

A: Oh, right, Professor Mackey. Sorry.

B: You should head over to the student affairs office right now. The sooner you get started on the application process, the better. And make sure your passport is current. You're definitely going to need that!

A: No problem. I just renewed it last month.

A

1. year
2. three
3. letter of recommendation
4. history
5. month

B

1.	Get a CLFE score of level 2.
2.	Get a letter of recommendation from a professor.
3.	Write a 500-word essay.
4.	Make sure your passport is current.

I heard you got your green card.

Listening p. 65

Script

A: Number 2-0-3, please. 2-0-3.

B: That's me.

A: How may I help you today?

B: Yes, I'd like to get a temporary work visa.

A: Okay. Do you have an application form and a letter from the company that is sponsoring your visa?

B: Yes, I do. They're right here.

A: Okay. Now in order to get your EAD, you'll need to submit a few more documents.

B: EAD? What's that?

A: EAD stands for employment authorization document. This is a permit that will allow you to work in the United States.

B: Yes, I see. That's what I need.

A: So what I need from you is a copy of your original birth certificate, a photo ID, and your passport.

B: Is my driver's license okay for the ID?

A: Yes, that's fine.

B: Okay. Here they are.

A: Great. It will take approximately four to six weeks to process your application, and we'll notify you when your EAD is ready.

B: How will you notify me?

A: We'll use the contact information on your application form.

B: Okay. Thank you very much.

A

1. a 2. a 3. b
4. c

B

1. True
2. False (driver's license → application form)
3. True

How do you like it here?

Listening p. 67

Script

1. Hi, I'm Marta. I work for a large bank in London. Life in England was difficult at first because I'm from Spain. But now I'm used to speaking the language, and I like it a lot. I'm a financial advisor. I help people choose the best ways to save their money. My bank offers lots of options, so it can be really difficult for customers to choose one. But I sit down and talk to them about their future plans. Then, I advise them on the best option. I start work at 8:30 a.m. and have a one-hour lunch break at 12:30 p.m. Then, I work again from 1:30 p.m. to 4:30 p.m. That's when my bank closes. I'm a people person, so I enjoy meeting with customers. But sometimes I have to fill out a lot of paperwork. I don't enjoy doing that very much. It's really boring.

2. Hey, I'm Shingo. I work for a telecommunications company in the United States. I'm a technician. I'm originally from Japan, but my family moved to the United States when I was ten. I work outside a lot because my job involves connecting wires to people's houses. I connect phone lines, cable lines, and Internet lines. It's hard work. In the summer, the heat is terrible. But in the winter, the cold is terrible, too. I like working outside in the spring and fall though. I start work at 7:00 a.m. and I have a half-hour lunch break at 11:00 a.m. Then, I work from 11:30 to 3:30 p.m. It's nice to finish early in the afternoon. I like to go to the gym after work.

3. Hey, guys! I'm Sunny. I live and work in Australia, but I'm actually from Korea. I work for a large multinational company in Sydney. I'm an accountant at the company. I love numbers! I've been working here for three years now. I graduated from university in Australia, and then I decided to find a job here instead of going back to my home country. I start work at 9:00 a.m., and I finish at 5:30 p.m. I get a 45-minute lunch break whenever I want to take it. My colleagues and I usually have lunch at 12:00 p.m. though. I love the beaches in Australia, and the weather is so warm. But I really miss my family, especially my sister. We are really close, so we talk on the phone almost every night.

A

1. False 2. False 3. False
4. True 5. False 6. True

B

	Marta	Shingo	Sunny
Country of origin	Spain	Japan	Korea
Country working in now	England	USA	Australia
Position at company	financial advisor	technician	accountant
Starting time	8:30 a.m.	7:00 a.m.	9:00 a.m.
Finish time	4:30 p.m.	3:30 p.m.	5:30 p.m.
Likes	meeting people	working outside in the spring and fall and finishing work early	numbers, beaches, and the weather
Dislikes	paperwork	hot and cold weather	missing family

Tips for Living Abroad

Reading p. 68

Comprehension Check

1. The staff at the Expat Handbook put them together.
2. They run to the familiar.
3. She lived in Thailand.
4. She suggests expats go to bookstores or online.
5. They can experience it by forming relationships with people from that culture.

Wrap-up p. 70

A

working holiday, visa, embassy, keep in touch

Unit 7 Dating

A Blind Date

Vocabulary p. 72

1. dating profile
2. starters
3. vegetarian
4. dessert
5. main course
6. sparkling water

Listening p. 73

Script

1. Hey, I'm Raoul. I've been very successful in the professional world. But I've never had much luck romantically. I'm looking to settle down, but I want to find someone who is a good match for me. I found MatchFinders online and decided to make a profile. I'm 34 years old, and I have an athletic, muscular build. I have dark brown hair and black eyes. I'm a businessman. I got my MBA from Harvard Business School. I got divorced two years ago. My ex and I share custody of our seven-year-old daughter, so I hope to find someone who likes kids. I like outdoor activities like skiing and playing tennis. I hate staying home and being lazy. I like to go out and do things. I'm not a smoker, nor am I much of a drinker. I'll have a glass of wine once in a while, but I really hate going to bars.

2. My name is Jessica. I'm 29 years old, and I go on dates quite often. But I haven't met the right guy yet. My friend Christa told me about MatchFinders.com. She met her boyfriend by using the dating site, and they've been together for two years. I have a chubby body. I have long red hair and blue eyes. I have a PhD in anthropology. I teach anthropology at a university in my city. I've been engaged, but I've never been married. I don't have any children although I'd really like to have some children in the future. I like outdoor activities, especially water sports like waterskiing and jet skiing. I don't like watching TV. It's such a waste of time. I'm not a smoker, and I drink alcohol occasionally. I like a glass of red wine on the weekend.

A

1. c
2. b
3. b
4. b

B

34	Age	29
MBA	Education	PhD
divorced	Marital Status	single
Yes	Children	No
skiing & tennis	Likes	water sports
stay home	Dislikes	TV

We're both in love.

Vocabulary p. 74

1. flirting with
2. crush
3. break up with
4. turnoff
5. love at first sight
6. turn-on

Listening p. 75

Script

In the digital age, dating is very different than it was in pre-Internet and pre-smartphone times. Online dating sites and dating apps might make meeting people easier, but there are some basic dos and don'ts about dating that never change. First, it's very important to make a good first impression. Remember to present yourself nicely because the other person will always remember that first meeting. In addition, meet in a location that's comfortable. Don't choose an event that is too formal, but also don't meet at a fast-food restaurant. That's too informal. Choose a place where you can relax and be yourself. Don't be shy on a first date. You don't want the other person to feel like he or she is carrying the whole conversation. But also be a good listener. Allow your partner to tell you about him or herself. Don't talk about serious topics like religion or politics. And never, ever talk about your exes. No one wants to hear about a partner's ex-boyfriend or ex-girlfriend. Remember to put your smartphone away. It's rude to be texting while on a first date. And finally, let the man pay for dinner. It's okay to be traditional. The man gets to feel like a prince, and the woman gets to feel like a princess.

A

1. Dating in the digital era is very different than the pre-Internet era.
2. People always remember a first meeting.
3. Don't choose an informal place like a fast-food restaurant.
4. Don't discuss topics like religion and politics.
5. Let the man pay.

B

Dating Dos and Don'ts
• Do make a good first impression. • Do meet in a place that's comfortable... not too formal / not too basic. • Don't be shy. • Do be a good listener. • Don't talk about your exes. • Don't stare at your smartphone the whole time.

She dumpled me.

Grammar p. 76

B

1. Sam said he had seen a car accident on his way to work today.
2. My parents said they were meeting the Millers at 7:00 p.m. on Tuesday.
3. Dr. Kristine said she was pleased with my presentation.
4. Chen said he had played tennis with her many times.

Listening p. 77

Script

1. A: Hello, Janelle speaking.
B: Janelle, this is Kathy.
A: Hi, Kathy. How are you?
B: Terrible.
A: What's wrong?
B: It's Charles.
A: What about Charles?
B: He's been lying to me. He said that he had gone to the gym this afternoon. But then I found a receipt in his pants pocket.
A: What kind of receipt?
B: He spent $5,000 at Tiffany's Jewelry. I don't think he even went to the gym. Why did he lie to me, Janelle? Why?
A: Oh, Kathy. I'm so sorry. He's a terrible husband.
B: I know. He is a terrible husband.

2. A: Hello?
B: Bill, this is Charles.
A: Hey, Char...
B: Shhhh! Is Janelle around?
A: No, she's upstairs on the phone.
B: Good. I need to ask you for a favor.
A: Sure, anything for you, Charles.
B: I need you and Janelle to babysit the children this evening.
A: Okay. Why?
B: I want to take Kathy to this new French restaurant called Le Café.
A: How romantic!
B: I'm going to give her this really expensive diamond bracelet from Tiffany's. But don't tell Janelle.
A: Why not?
B: It's Kathy's birthday next week, and I want it to be a surprise.
A: Got it. I won't say a thing.
B: Thanks, Bill.
A: No problem, Charles. You're a great husband. Kathy's a lucky woman.
B: You think so?
A: Absolutely.
B: Yeah. I am a great husband.

A

1. b 2. b 3. a
4. c 5. b

Script

A: Who were you talking to?
B: That was Charles.
A: Charles? What did he want?
B: Nothing. He just wanted to chat. Who were you talking to?
A: Kathy. She's really upset.
B: Upset? Why?
A: Charles said that he had gone to the gym this afternoon. But he lied. Kathy found a jewelry store receipt in his pants pocket. Boy, he's such a...
B: No, it's not what you think.
A: What do you mean?
B: It's a secret. I'm not supposed to tell you.
A: Kathy's my best friend. You had better tell me everything this second.
B: Okay, okay. Charles bought some jewelry for Kathy. It's a surprise birthday gift. He's going to give it to her next week.
A: Oh, no. I have to tell Kathy.
B: No, you can't. It's a surprise. I wasn't supposed to tell you.

Dating and Technology

Reading p. 78

Comprehension Check

1. They had to ask them out face to face.
2. They send text messages.
3. They can avoid the discomfort of rejection or rejecting someone.
4. He believes we are in a transitional moment. Dating norms are changing.
5. He thinks rejection can be a good thing.

Wrap-up p. 80

A

1. Simon said he was watching the baseball game.
2. Yoon and Ganghyeok said they had been to Paris.
3. Ella said she had gone on a date with Brian last weekend.
4. Effie and Tony said they were going to stay in Finland before going to South Korea.

B

1. love at first sight
2. broke up
3. crush
4. flirting with
5. turnoff

Unit 8 Traffic

There must have been an accident.

Vocabulary p. 82

1. fine
2. route
3. sirens
4. pedestrians
5. bumper to bumper
6. residential

Listening p. 83

Script

Hi, my name's Ian Bloom. I'm a traffic signal coordinator. I work for the city of Milwaukee, Wisconsin. My job is to ensure that traffic moves smoothly in our city, especially during the rush hour periods of 7 to 9 a.m. and 4:30 to 6:30 p.m. Not many people know about this job. In fact, many people think traffic lights operate by computer only. But that's not exactly the case. Computers send information about traffic to our office. We use this information, as well as charts, maps, and graphs, to tell us how to coordinate traffic. For example, we need to know how long we should let the busiest streets' traffic lights remain green. This way, we can keep the flow of traffic moving and avoid traffic congestion, or traffic jams. During a particularly heavy day of traffic, we must do our best to keep traffic flowing. If there's an accident, we must make traffic flow to alternate routes that avoid the intersection where the accident occurred. My job can be very stressful because peoples' safety depends on it. That is why I have a team of five people working for me during the week. Although this job is stressful, it's nice knowing that we helped people get to work and get home safely.

A

1. c
2. b
3. c
4. c

B

1. True
2. False
3. False
4. True

I see a free space right there!

Vocabulary p. 84

A

1. car vandalism
2. jaywalking
3. texting while driving
4. illegal parking
5. speeding
6. running a red light
7. drunk driving
8. getting pulled over

Listening p. 85

Script

1. A: Hello, ma'am. Do you know why I pulled you over?
   B: No, I don't. Was I speeding?
   A: No, that's not the problem. I saw you using your phone. We have strict laws against the use of electronic devices while driving in this county.
   B: Oh, I wasn't texting. I was using my phone's navigation system.
   A: That may be true. However, if you want to use your phone's navigation system, it must be mounted on your dashboard. You can't hold it in your hand.
   B: Oh, no. I didn't know that. Are you going to give me a ticket?
   A: Yes, I am.
2. A: Good morning, sir. Do you know why I pulled you over?
   B: No, not really.
   A: You ran that red light about 300 meters back.
   B: Which red light?
   A: It was at the intersection of Rose Street and New Haven Boulevard.
   B: I don't think I did. It was yellow.
   A: No, it was definitely red. My patrol car camera caught the whole incident.
   B: Really?
   A: Yes. Please give me your license and registration.
   B: Okay. Here you are.

1. a
2. c
3. a
4. a

Writing a Police Report p. 85

POLICE REPORT

Date *Halloween last year*

Time *5:30 P.M.*

Place of Incident *At the intersection of Elk Drive and Riverside Place*

Details of Event *A tan four-door sedan ran a red light and hit a cyclist who was crossing the street.*

Actions Taken *Officer Gary Pittman interviewed the driver and the cyclist and determined that the driver was at fault. The driver was ticketed and fined for running a red light. The driver was also asked to replace the bicycle he damaged in the accident. The driver agreed to buy the cyclist a new bicycle.*

I got a flat tire.

Useful Expressions p. 86

A

1. c 2. e 3. a
4. d 5. b 6. f

Listening p. 87

Script

A: So which one do you like more?
B: I kind of like the blue station wagon.
A: Why?
B: It's newer than the van. It's the 2015 model, but the van is a 2014 model.
A: But the van has more kilometers on it.
B: How many kilometers does it have on it?
A: It has 85,000 kilometers.
B: How many does the wagon have?
A: It only has 50,000 kilometers.
B: Hmm. The van is more expensive though. It's $18,000. The hatchback is only $13,000. That's a big difference.
A: But the van is so much roomier. It would be great for the kids, especially for driving them to and from soccer practice. It would also be so good for grocery shopping.
B: You really like the van, don't you?
A: I do. Can we please buy it?
B: Okay, let's do it.

A

1. station wagon 2. children
3. roomier 4. van
5. van

B

• Car Type: van • Year: 2014 • Price: $18,000 • Kilometers: 85,000	• Car Type: station wagon • Year: 2015 • Price: $13,000 • Kilometers: 50,000

The Car of the Future

Reading p. 88

Comprehension Check

1. They will have Internet connectivity.
2. They will not be installed.
3. Many will be self-driving.
4. The cities have too much pollution.

Wrap-up p. 90

A

1. so much traffic that are very close together and can hardly move
2. the way between two places along which buses, planes, or ships travel regularly
3. a punishment in which a person is ordered to pay due to his or her doing something illegal or breaking a rule
4. a person who is walking
5. A residential area contains houses rather than offices or factories.
6. a warning device which makes a long and loud noise
7. making somebody or something move to the side of the road and stop
8. the act of walking across a street in a careless and dangerous way or not at the proper place

Unit 9 The Environment and Volunteer Work

We reuse one-sided copies.

Vocabulary p. 92

1. reusable 2. recycling bins
3. compost 4. aluminum
5. waste 6. paper shredder
7. energy efficient 8. trash bag

Listening p. 93

Script

Hey, guys! It's Vanessa here with another video. I've got a question for all my YouBlog fans out there. I want to talk to you about a problem I have in my office. I don't think we do a very good job of recycling. Our breakroom only has one large trash bin in there, and everybody throws their garbage into that bin.

It doesn't matter if the garbage is a soda can, a juice bottle, or half of a sandwich. It all gets thrown out in the evening. I'm afraid that trash will never get recycled and will end up in a landfill somewhere. I'm getting really tired of seeing such disrespect for the environment, and I want to say something to my co-workers, but I'm scared. I mean, what if they get angry at me or call me a hypocrite? I don't recycle when I'm at work. I do at home, but at work, I behave just like everybody else. If you have any good suggestions, please leave comments in the comments section. I'd love to read them. Thanks! Byeee!

A

1. a	2. b	3. a
4. b		

Script

Hey, guys! It's Vanessa again. Thanks for all of your comments. Some of them were more helpful than others, but I appreciate all of your replies. I want to especially thank Earthangel. I talked to our office manager at work, and she thought it was a great idea to buy different colored trash bins. I even went to the hardware store with her to pick out the bins. The new system has been working great, and I found out that the cleaning staff really loves it, too. They had been separating the recyclable items from the garbage each night after work. Now they no longer have to do that, so it saves them a lot of time. Thanks again and best wishes to all my viewers. See you soon! Byeee!

C

Summary: Vanessa felt bad because the workers in her office were not recycling their waste. She made a YouBlog video about her problem. In the video, she asked for solutions to the problem. One commenter, named Earthangel, gave her some good advice, and now the problem in her office has been solved.

I hate that car alarm!

Vocabulary p. 94

1. contamination, b	2. nutrients, chemicals, c
3. atmosphere, d	4. mutative, radioactive, a

Listening p. 95

Script

A: Hey, Maria! What are you reading?

B: It's an article in *Healthy Lifestyle Magazine*.

A: What's the article about?

B: It's about the health effects of light pollution.

A: Light pollution? What's that?

B: It's when too much unnatural light is emitted in an area. It happens a lot in big cities.

A: How does it affect us?

B: Our eyes receive too much light at night. The light disrupts our natural sleep patterns.

A: It does?

B: Yeah. Our bodies have this thing called a circadian rhythm. The circadian rhythm keeps our bodies in a natural state of sleep and wakefulness. The problem is that in big cities, there's a lot of unnatural light being emitted at all times. The light hitting our eyes upsets the natural sleep cycle.

A: You mean our bodies think it's day when it's actually night?

B: Exactly. And it's really unhealthy.

A: It is?

B: Yeah. One of the most important purposes of sleep is cellular repair. During the day, our cells are damaged by the sun, the food we eat, exercise, and other activities. But sleep helps our bodies repair that cell damage naturally. However, not sleeping or getting bad sleep means the cell damage is not being repaired properly.

A: What can I do to prevent this cell damage?

B: You need to get good, restful sleep. The writer suggests not using your smartphone or watching TV for at least an hour before going to sleep. And buy thick curtains that block out all of the light in your bedroom. She says that for most people, the darker the room is, the better the sleep is.

A: That's great information, Maria, Thanks.

B: No problem, Matt.

A

1. c	2. c	3. a
4. c	5. b	6. a

B

1. False	2. True	3. False
4. False		

We're going to clean up a park.

Listening p. 97

Script

Good morning, InfoTech employees. I appreciate the fact that you took time out of your busy schedules to join me in the auditorium today. After several months of discussion, we have finally chosen a volunteer project that we think is a good fit with the InfoTech brand and will do lots of good in the community. We are going to dedicate the next six weeks to renovating the community youth center. As you know, the city's youth center has fallen into disrepair due to budgetary constraints. We would like to solve that problem by supplying the materials and personnel necessary to bring the community center back to an acceptable level of decency so the children in the community can enjoy it. The company has dedicated $50,000 to pay for supplies such as paint, wood, furniture, and games such as table tennis and billiards. We will also provide the tools necessary to complete the project although if you are more comfortable using your own tools, that's fine, too. Work will start on Saturday, July 7th, and should be completed by September 2nd. We need no fewer than 50 volunteers each Saturday. We have decided that volunteers who give up a Saturday to work on the project will be eligible for the company raffle. First prize in the raffle will be a new 2018 Arizona sports utility vehicle. We kindly ask that you volunteer for at least one of the six Saturdays; however, the more Saturdays you volunteer, the better chance you have to win the top prize. Each day you volunteer buys you one raffle ticket. If you're interested in signing up for our volunteer project, please talk to Cameron and Michaela after the meeting. Thanks and have a great day.

A

1. The company is going to dedicate the next six weeks to the project.
2. The city has budget constraints.
3. Volunteers can bring their own tools to the project.
4. The company will pay for table tennis tables and billiards.
5. Raffle tickets will be given to all of the volunteers.

B

InfoTech Volunteer Project	
Type of Project	renovating the community youth center
Number of Volunteers	at least 50 per day
Location	community youth center
Budget	$50,000
Starting Date	July 7th
Finish date	September 2nd

Voluntourism

Reading p. 98

Comprehension Check

1. It's going to another country to help people and to travel.
2. You get to decide.
3. The articles cite architects, plumbers, electricians, construction workers.
4. The project manager will show the volunteers the city.
5. They take appointments with interested people.

Wrap-up p. 100

A

1. aluminum
2. waste
3. paper shredder
4. energy efficient
5. recycling bins
6. compost
7. reusable
8. trash bag

Unit 10 Fine Arts

Warm-up p. 101

1. threatening, gloomy, miserable, depressing, anxious
2. colorful, comfortable, pleasant, peaceful, romantic

This is amazing!

Vocabulary p. 102

1. painting
2. drawing / sketch
3. sculpture
4. photograph
5. portrait
6. abstract
7. graffiti
8. architecture

Listening p. 103

Script

A: I like this one. It's really beautiful.

B: It's very famous.

A: Who painted it?

B: It was painted by Claude Monet.

A: It looks old?

B: It's pretty old. It was painted in the late 1800s. 1875. I think.

A: What's the story behind this painting?

B: It's called *Woman with a Parasol*. The woman is Monet's wife Camille. And the child in the background is their son Jean.

A: It's simple but beautiful.

B: Monet's paintings often involved simple scenes like this. He painted people in parks or in a boat on a pond.

A: The style is unique.

B: It's called Impressionism.

A: What's Impressionism?

B: It's a style created by French painters in the late 19th century. The short brushstrokes imitate light reflecting off objects.

A: The colors are so bright.

B: That's right. Bright colors and short brushstrokes are two of the most prominent features of Impressionism. At the time, Impressionism was not taken seriously. But now these paintings are sold for millions of dollars.

A

1. c
2. a
3. c
4. a

B

1. True
2. False
3. True

Venus of Willendorf

Crossword Puzzle p. 104

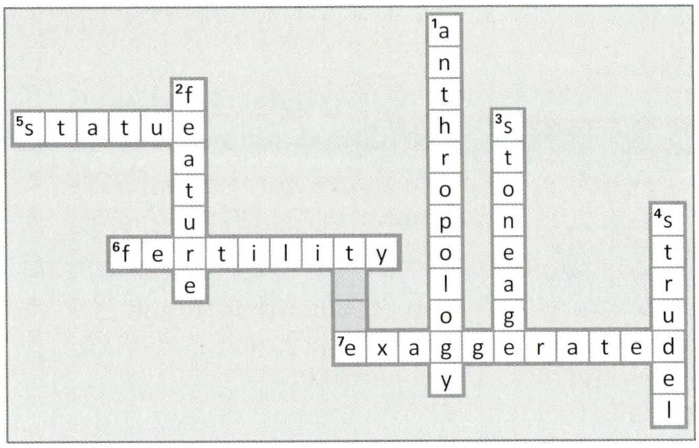

Listing p. 105

Script

Okay, now this next piece is called *The Starry Night*, and it was painted by none other than the Dutch impressionist painter Vincent van Gogh in 1889. It is one of the most famous pieces in the New York Metropolitan Museum of Art. The painting depicts the view of the night sky just before sunrise from the second-floor window of the Saint Paul de Mausole Lunatic Asylum. You see, Van Gogh had checked himself into the mental hospital after cutting off his ear and giving it to his love interest, a prostitute at a local brothel. At least, that's what we've been led to believe all these years. What's interesting about this story is that it may not be entirely true. Recently, two German art historians published a book that casts doubt on the previous story. The new description of events comes from letters written by Van Gogh and his friend Paul Gauguin, who was present the night Van Gogh lost a piece of his ear. You see, the authors theorize that Van Gogh became aggressive toward Gauguin one night, forcing Gauguin to defend himself. Instead of killing his friend, Gauguin, an expert fencer, slashed Van Gogh's ear. Horrified and scared by the incident, Gauguin left his friend's house and the city immediately. Van Gogh never spoke publicly about the incident because he didn't want his friend to get arrested. Shortly after this event, Van Gogh checked himself into the mental hospital. It was at the hospital that he created some of his most famous paintings. Although they had been good friends before Van Gogh's injury, the two men never saw each other again.

A

1. b 2. b 3. c
4. c

B

Title of Artwork: *The Starry Night*	
Artist's Name	Vincent van Gogh
Style	Impressionism
Year	1889
Museum	NY MoMA (New York Metropolitan Museum of Art)

Street Art

Listening p. 107

Script

My absolute favorite architect is Frank Lloyd Wright. His most brilliant work, the Fallingwater Home, pictured here, is a perfect example of organic architecture, a term that was coined to describe his style of architecture. Wright was probably the best-known American architect and made a lasting impression on architecture by inspiring generations of architects over the past 70 years. In this amazing example, you can see how well the home has been integrated into the natural surroundings. This home was built over a waterfall in Southwestern Pennsylvania, USA. All of the angles and shapes are in harmony with the stream and the trees. It's almost as if the house grew naturally from its environment. Wright's style is actually in stark contrast to the trends that were popular at the time this house was built in 1935. In the 1930s, architecture was about conquering the natural environment by building amazing structures like the great skyscrapers of New York City. Those structures pulled people's attention away from nature and focused it on the unnatural, albeit amazing, manmade buildings. A prime example of this is the Empire State Building. When domination over the natural environment was the status quo, Wright went in the opposite direction, designing structures that were functional, beautiful, and in harmony with the environment. And that is why he is considered a hero in the architecture community to this day.

A

1. Frank Lloyd Wright's work has inspired younger generations for the past 70 years.
2. Wright's structures are in harmony with the environment.
3. Architecture was about conquering the environment in the 1930s.
4. The Empire State Building is not an example of organic architecture.
5. Wright went in the opposite direction as his generation of architects.

B

Architect	Frank Lloyd Wright
Name of Structure	*Fallingwater Home*
Year	1935
Location	Southwestern Pennsylvania, USA
Style	Organic architecture

Art Quiz p. 107

1. Spring Temple Buddha in China
2. Damien Hirst
3. France
4. Simple scenes, bright colors, and short brushstrokes imitating light reflecting off objects

A Strange Contest

Reading p. 108

Comprehension Check

1. It was expected to raise $20 million.
2. Both auction houses were well respected.
3. He wanted them to play rock, scissors, paper.
4. They thought the other side would choose paper.

Wrap-up p. 110

A

1. g 2. e 3. c
4. b 5. f 6. a
7. d 8. h

Unit 11 Healthy Life Habits

Tell me about your diet and lifestyle.

Listening p. 113

Script

A: Melissa, you look great. How did you get so thin?

B: I read a book by Dr. John Erickson called *Eat to Live*. It changed my life.

A: *Eat to Live*? I know that book. It's on the *New York Times* bestseller's list.

B: That's right. It's the most sensible book on deting I've ever read. He explains nutrition so simply. When I read it, something just clicked for me.

A: What's the gist of it?

B: He explains that humans are eating too many animal products these days. We need to get back to a plant-based diet.

A: Oh, so you're a vegetarian now.

B: No, not at all. It's about changing the foundation of your diet. I still eat meat.

A: Then what's the foundation of your diet now?

B: It depends on where you live, but for most people following Dr. Erickson's principles, vegetables, especially dark green leafy vegetables, are the foundation of the diet. I eat a lot of lettuce, kale, and broccoli.

A: That's cool. I love broccoli.

B: Me, too. And then you can build on that with other vegetables, nuts, and seeds and some fruit. You can even put some chicken breast or turkey in your salad. I also like to make my own balsamic vinaigrette dressing. It's sugar-free, of course.

A: So you're eating a lot of salads.

B: I am. But it's not boring at all. If you take the time to prepare them right, salads are absolutely delicious.

A: How much weight have you lost?

B: In total, I've lost 15 kilograms. But my goal is to lose another five.

A: Well you look great!

B: Thanks.

A: Okay, you've convinced me. I'm going to order a copy of the book today.

B: No need. You can borrow mine.

A

1. c 2. c 3. b
4. a

B

1. True 2. False 3. False
4. True 5. True

I'm in!

Words Search Puzzle p. 114

1. b 2. c 3. a
4. f 5. e 6. d

e	n	w	o	r	k	o	u	t	c
x	s	w	q	f	e	k	j	w	o
a	a	o	j	h	q	q	s	h	m
c	f	r	l	j	u	o	k	u	m
t	w	k	c	h	i	p	i	n	e
l	e	s	h	a	p	e	b	d	r
y	q	h	g	f	m	p	q	e	c
f	z	e	u	l	e	a	f	s	i
q	s	e	q	w	n	x	s	n	a
k	h	t	k	z	t	d	m	e	l

Listening p. 115

Script

A: So, Michael, I reviewed your online survey, and I put together an exercise and nutrition plan for you. Let's start with your diet. Your average daily caloric intake is 3,000 calories. That's too many. As a 40-year-old adult who is 180cm tall, you should be consuming no more than 1,800 calories per day.

B: I eat too much then?

A: Yes, I think overeating has contributed to your weight problem. I'd also like to see you stop eating processed foods and simple carbohydrates such as bread and pasta. Those foods offer very little nutrition and are high in calories.

B: But they taste so good.

A: I know. Those foods are designed to taste good, but if you want to be healthy, you really have to avoid them. I want you to get most of your calories from fresh vegetables and fruit. And I don't want you to consume any soda or fruit juice. Those items contain only empty calories.

B: Okay. I drink a lot of juice. I'm going to stop buying it.

A: Good. And I'd like you to start exercising.

B: I play basketball every Saturday.

A: That's good, but you need more exercise than that. I want you to do thirty minutes of cardio three times a week. That could be a thirty-minute walk, hike, or bike ride.

B: Okay, I can do that.

A: And I want you to lift weights three times a week. Lifting weights will keep your bones healthy as you get older.

B: I do ten pushups every morning.

A: That's just not enough. I want you to build muscle in your lower body and upper body.

B: Okay, thank you, Doctor.

A: You're welcome. I'd like to see you again in my office three months from now so we can assess your progress.

B: Of course. See you in three months.

A

1. Michael is 40 years old and 180cm tall.
2. The doctor would like to see Michael stop eating processed foods.
3. Michael drinks a lot of juice.
4. Michael plays basketball on Saturdays.
5. Michael will see the doctor three months from now.

B

	Michael's Lifestyle Now	New Health Plan for Michael
Number of Calories	3000	1800
Diet	processed foods and carbohydrates	fresh vegetables and fruit
Cardio Exercise	basketball on Saturdays	30 minutes of cardio three times a week
Weightlifting	ten pushups every morning	lifting weights three times a week

How do you meditate?

Vocabulary p. 116

1. cool, peaceful, tranquil
2. anxious, nervous, tense
3. dog-tired, fatigued, tired

Listening p. 117

Script

A: Okay, now I want you to relax, Cassandra. Feel all of life's daily annoyances wash away like an ocean wave. See the wave getting smaller and smaller in the distance. Can you see the wave?

B: Yes, I can.

A: Good. Imagine a beautiful place, anywhere on Earth. What do you see?

B: I see beautiful white clouds.

A: Good. What time of day is it?

B: It's midday. The sun is shining brightly.

A: Do you see a green field?

B: No.

A: Are there mountains or a lake?

B: No, but there's water, lots of water.

A: Is the water clear?

B: No, it's blue. The water is very blue.

A: Is there sand?

B: Yes, there's beautiful white sand.

A: Good. Now I want you to breathe and count backward from five. Are you ready?

B: 5 – 4 – 3 – 2 – 1.

A: Now wake up.

B: Oh, wow. That was amazing. Why did you stop?

A: Your session is over. That'll be thirty-five dollars, please.

B: Thirty-five dollars?

A: That's right. You can pay the receptionist, Amanda, in the lobby. We accept VISA, Mastercard, and cash. No personal checks, please.

B: Can I make another appointment?

A: Of course. You can schedule another appointment with Amanda.

B: Oh... okay. Bye, Dr. Mark.

A: Goodbye, Cassandra.

A

1. Dr. Mark's office accepts credit cards and cash.
2. The woman must pay Amanda directly.
3. The person who receives payments is the same person who schedules appointments.

B

4

Meditating p. 117

Script

You are about to experience an incredible sense of calmness and serenity. Your eyes are closed, and your mind is free to wander. You are standing in a beautiful place surrounded by people or things that bring you the most happiness in life. A soft wind blows through your hair. You feel the soft, cool breeze on your face. In the distance, the sun begins to set on the horizon. The sky is majestic shades of yellows, oranges, and pinks. You lie on the soft ground and gaze at the clouds as they move slowly across the sky. You breathe the fresh, cool air into your lungs and then exhale. You open your eyes. You feel relaxed and peaceful.

I'm a yoga teacher.

Reading p. 118

Comprehension Check

1. She teaches in the morning, afternoon, and evenings.
2. People of all ages and genders are doing yoga these days.
3. It was really difficult. It almost killed her.
4. A family friend helped her open the business.

Wrap-up p. 120

A

1. peaceful
2. chip in
3. post-workout journals

Unit 12 Lucky Me!

I've won!

Listening p. 123

Script

A: What are we going to do?

B: I don't know. How much is our monthly house payment?

A: It's $750. And our utilities are $200 per month.

B: What's our food budget?

A: I've only budgeted $200 a month for food. And that's tight.

B: Your and my car payments are $600 a month, right?

A: No! They're $700 in total. And we have to pay $1,200 every six months for car insurance.

B: Oh, boy. How much do I earn after taxes?

A: Your job only pays $1,900 per month after taxes. We're short $150.00 every month. What are we going to do?

B: I don't know. Maybe you could get a part-time job.

A: How am I going to work and go to school full time? It's just not possible. Graduate school requires all of my time and energy right now.

B: Okay, I understand. Hmm... I don't know what we're going to do. Can we ask your parents?

A: No, way! I'm not asking them for any more money.

B: Hold on a sec. Let me answer this call.

A

1. b 2. b 3. c
4. b

Script

A: Mhmm... mhmm... yes... Thank you, sir. Yes, I understand. Thank you very much. Okay, now. Goodbye.

B: Who was that?

A: That was my boss.

B: Is everything okay?

A: Everything is better than okay.

B: Tell me. What did he say?

A: He offered me a promotion.

B: What? Are you kidding?

A: No, I'm not kidding. He wants me to transfer to the corporate office downtown.

B: That's closer to our house.

A: I know! And that's not all. He wants to put me on the management track. He said I could become a general manager of a store within five years.

B: That's amazing. What about right now?

A: I'll be learning the ins and outs of the corporate system. I'll be working on a team led by a regional manager.

B: What about the pay? Does it pay more?

A: It sure does. It pays an extra $200 per week.

B: Aaaahh! That's amazing. We are so lucky.

A: I know.

B

1. False 2. False 3. False
4. True

What a horrible day!

Listening p. 125

Script

1. Hey, I'm Tim. This happened to me about twenty years ago. I had just graduated from university and was starting my first real job at a large company downtown. On my first day of work, I arrived early and found a parking spot near the entrance. I said to myself, "Wow! How lucky is that? It must be a sign." Oh, it was a sign all right. At about 9:30 a.m.

my boss entered the office. He was screaming and yelling, and his face was bright red. I asked my co-worker what was wrong. He told me that someone had parked in his assigned parking space and that the parking lot attendants were trying to track down the driver. When I heard this, a chill went down my spine. Just then, my boss called me into his office. He yelled at me for half an hour. Needless to say, I didn't last long at that job. And I learned to read the signs carefully before parking somewhere. Oh, what a horrible day that was.

2. Hi there! My name's Angela, and my story occurred about three years ago. I can laugh about this situation now, but at the time, it was awful. I was on a business trip in London, England. I had gone there to meet with an important client. The purpose of my visit was to give a sales presentation about our company's new product lines. The presentation usually took about 30 minutes, and there were lots of slides with graphs, charts, tables, and, of course, pictures. My presentation was supposed to start at 10:00 a.m., so I left my hotel at 9:30 a.m. By 9:45, I was in the boardroom ready to give the presentation when I realized that I had left my USB drive at the hotel. People had already begun filing into the boardroom. I started panicking. Sweat was dripping down my forehead. Then, the big boss came in. There was nothing I could do but to give the presentation the old-fashioned way: without slides. Of course, we didn't get the account, and I didn't get the promotion I had been hoping for. I learned a tough lesson that day. Always back up your files because you never know when you might forget something.

3. Hey, I'm Ryan, and something really unlucky happened to me last week. My girlfriend broke up with me about a month ago. We had been dating for almost three years. Anyway, I was alone and feeling down on a Friday night, so I called my best friend and asked him if he wanted to see a movie. I thought it would help me stop thinking about my ex-girlfriend for a couple of hours. We arrived at the theater and got in line. We were just chatting in line when I suddenly spotted my ex-girlfriend near the front of the line. But that's not the whole story; she was with another guy and they were holding hands. Ugh! We had only been broken up like three weeks at the time, and she was already dating some new guy. Luckily, she didn't see us. My friend and I slipped into a new line and out of sight of my ex. We ended up watching a different movie that was just terrible. My friend tried to cheer me up, but I was just miserable. Why did I have to see my ex-girlfriend?

A

1. False (late → early)
2. True
3. False (forty-five minutes → thirty minutes)
4. False (office → hotel)
5. True
6. False (back → front)

B

	Tim	Angela	Ryan
Where	at work	in the boardroom	at the theater
When	twenty years ago	three years ago	last week
What Happened	He parked his car in his boss's assigned parking space.	She left her USB drive at the hotel and ruined her presentation.	He saw his ex-girlfriend going out on a date.

Luck vs. Attitude

Reading p. 128

Comprehension Check

1. Luck is actually a set of behaviors.
2. They create opportunities, they don't quit, and they are optimistic.
3. They never gave up even when things looked bleak.
4. People will also find success.

Wrap-up p. 130

A

lottery, gambling, a lucky break, fortune